Mum Hacks

Mum Hacks

Time-saving tips to calm the chaos
of family life

Tanith Carey

white
LADDER

This first e

19–21c Cha

Previously   an

Amazing   Handbook

for Hassle   ng has

been fully

© Crimson Publishing 2016

British Library Cataloguing in Publication Data
A catalogue record for this book is available from the British Library

ISBN 9781910336229

Typeset by IDSUK (DataConnection) Ltd
Printed and bound in the UK by Ashford Colour Press, Gosport, Hants
Cover design and illustrations © www.ninataradesign.com

Contents

About the author

Tanith Carey is an award-winning journalist and author, who writes for a variety of publications, including *The Daily Telegraph*, the *Guardian* and the *Daily Mail*. She has written eight books and regularly appears on TV and radio to help address the most pressing issues for today's modern parents. She lives with her husband and two daughters in London.

Acknowledgements

Along with the many mums, educators, nutritionists, foodies, life coaches and beauty and exercise experts who shared their knowledge and experience with me, thanks should also go to Noël Janis-Norton, Beth Bishop, Kate Kirkpatrick, Lucy Cogan, and Anthony, Lily and Clio Harwood.

Introduction

When you first held your new-born baby in your arms, did you make a promise to be the best possible parent you could be? In the years that stretched before you, did you imagine always saying the right thing, listening when your child chattered, and always having the time to sit down and play? Then, somewhere along the way, did being 'busy' get in the way of the parent you hoped to be? Gradually, did child-raising start to feel like an unwinnable race against a stop-watch: always in a panic, always late, with everything never quite under your control?

If this sounds like you, you're not alone. There is no experience more relentless or all-consuming than being a parent.

When I had my first baby, Lily, like every other mother I was utterly shocked by how much multi-tasking it involved. I'd tidy up the house, but as fast as I could pick up toys, Lily would throw them on the floor. She'd tell me she was hungry and then didn't want to eat what I'd cook. I'd give her everything she asked for – and she would dream up something else. With no family support and a partner who worked very long hours, I found myself on my own and unable to even go to the loo without my daughter wanting to sit on my lap.

If the job of raising a child is not challenging enough by itself, there's also the fact that many more of us now combine child-rearing with working.

The number of families who need two wage-earners to own a home and keep up with the cost of living in the UK has hit a record high, with 2.25 million women with children under four already back at work.[1] Another two million parents are raising kids alone.[2] On top of that, economic uncertainty, the 'long hours' culture and the creeping tendrils of technology, which allows work to follow us home, mean that people in the UK work longer days than any other nation in Europe. The result is that 87% of British employees say they feel stressed – nearly twice the European average.[3]

But it's not just adults who are feeling it.

A quarter of all parents say that long days and lengthy commutes mean that they spend just 34 undistracted minutes a day with their children.[4] One in five report they are too tired to even read their kids a bedtime story – even though it's one of the most bonding moments of the day.[5] The knock-on effect is naturally felt by our children. Shockingly, six out of 10 children say that they don't think their parents spend enough time with them. When asked about the grown-ups in their lives, what they want most is for adults to be less stressed and less tired from work.[6]

It's no surprise, then, that the number of kids who say they would like to spend more time playing with their parents increased from 38% in 2009 to 47% in 2014.[7] After all, it's no longer just the dash to work. Every morning harried grown-ups can be seen sprinting behind buggies, bringing bewildered-looking babies and toddlers to nurseries and childminders before they can set off to work. The same cortisol-inducing exercise is then repeated in the evening when many parents have to peel off from work to pick up their offspring before tight deadlines to dodge late fees. The extended family which once helped spread the load has been broken up, so all too often there is little support or help.

Even if parents do work from home – as they increasingly do to try to claw back some time with their kids – children often get even more directly exposed to work stress. Many work-at-home parents will have noticed that, as if by magic, they get the most critical calls and emails towards the end of the day as office-based staff clear their to-do lists. So often the timing seems to coincide with the period between pick-up and bedtime, when parents had hoped to be there for their kids. Bosses with urgent queries rarely worry about the domino effect on the tension levels in the family home. That's your problem. Not theirs.

Pulled in every direction, many of today's working parents spend most of their time feeling burnt out and struggling to keep the show on the road. Imagine how scary it must be for a child, who relies on his parents for everything, to see them being overwhelmed. In our drive to support our little ones and provide for them materially, it's easy to forget that anxiety is contagious and that we, the parents, set the emotional thermostat in our homes.

Animal and human studies find that when parents are stressed, their offspring are too.[8] Baby rats, for example, are more fearful and hyper-vigilant if their mothers are too busy to lick them and calm them down. In humans, babies who sense their parents' anxiety feel more pain from injections, studies have found.[9] In our manic rush, we miss the fact that children from stressed families often process all this by feeling they are to blame. Our unhappiness leads them to believe that we don't like them very much.

According to Professor David Elkind, a child psychologist and professor at Tufts University, Massachusetts, 'Young children tend to perceive hurrying as a rejection, as evidence their parents do not really care about them.' Beyond this, stress overload is quite simply the greatest enemy there is of good parenting. It makes us forget our best intentions and turns us reactive and panicky, especially when all does not go to plan. Adrenalin makes every setback feel more serious and makes every reaction more knee-jerk.[10]

When we are in a wired state, anything a child does 'wrong' seems more wilful and deliberately antagonistic. Without the vocabulary or life experience to understand how they feel, children are more likely to react by playing up or disconnecting, raising the tension levels in the home still further. Our parenting becomes less empathetic and more impatient. We are so busy keeping ourselves afloat that all we want is our kids to comply without question. At other times, our standards slip – we become inconsistent in applying them and we opt for 'anything for a quiet life' parenting. Routines that provide safety and security go out of the window, and there end up being more rows about homework and bedtimes. Without realising it, we can get frustrated that we seem to spend our lives in our children's service, and then even more frustrated that they seem to us to want still more, and behave worse, creating a true vicious circle.

As a parenting journalist, in the privileged position of being able to talk to a wide range of educators, psychologists, teachers and parents and help join the dots on the bigger picture, I have seen the trickle-down effect. All of my parenting books to date have looked at the effect the current environment has on children's mental health. Modern life may be evolving at a breakneck speed, but our children still need the same things to become emotionally healthy adults. At a time when parents have never grappled with so many time pressures, I wrote this book because we all need help to keep up our connection with our kids, which seems to be increasingly under threat in a busy world. Beyond that, I have also been here myself.

Like most other mums (a recent survey found that on average, we perform 59 separate tasks a day to run a home and care for children[11]) I became like the White Rabbit in *Alice in Wonderland*, noticing only the time, instead of the life that was passing me by. Indeed, my least favourite memory of being a parent was when my six-year-old daughter Lily lay prostrate on the floor as I tried to send an urgent email (my computer had crashed) while she screamed, 'You said you'd play with me!' When I had my second child, instead of finding it easier, I found the workload more than doubled.

Yet even though it was becoming obvious that there was an epidemic of exhausted parents out there, I was amazed to see that despite the shelves of books saying how to be a good parent, not one addressed how to find the *time* to be that parent in the first place.

So I started to make a conscious effort to find ways to cut out the irritating distractions, frustrations and lost minutes that were making the hard job of being a working mother even harder. I researched ways to streamline and simplify the dozens of tasks I needed to do every day – 'life hacks', if you will. I also spoke to other mums and experts for a range of articles on the subject, and tried and tested them all.

Many parents will try to get through the ongoing mayhem on the assumption that things will get better soon. But as family educator Rob Parsons of Care for the Family once so poignantly pointed out, 'A slower day is not coming.'[12]

Let me stress now: this is not a book about rushing your children. Nothing could be more counter-productive. Hurrying kids only makes them needier and more demanding. It may sound corny, but the truth is that children really do spell LOVE as TIME.

But while you will never have more hours in the day, you do have the power to prioritise and make better use of the hours you do have. In a world that has become increasingly complex and time-consuming – and the bar for parenting has become unrealistically high – sometimes we need to take a step back in order to see how to simplify our lives. This is what this book is about.

The good news is that it is never too late to streamline your tasks and relax a little. By feeling less overwhelmed you will be able to quickly adjust the emotional temperature in your home. Indeed, the effects will be instantaneous.

As you read through this book, it may seem counter-intuitive that some small and minor changes could make any difference. But this book is also designed to be cumulative. These tips and strategies are designed to be easy to build into your life as you go along. From how to get out of the house on time in the morning without the melt-downs – so that you can start the day in a more relaxed frame of mind – to choosing children's clothes that are easier to launder, the goal is to help you feel that you are winning a bit more, and under the cosh a bit less.

Furthermore, the last thing I want is for you to be working any harder than you already are. So any costs I suggest are minimal, optional or designed to help you look at any new product you need to buy, like a high chair or dishwasher, more clearly in terms of whether it will simplify your life and how much time it will save you. You are probably reading this book because you already feel that you don't have enough minutes in the day. So there are no complicated lists to fill out or six-week action plans to add to your already-loaded to-do list.

Don't feel the book is just for mums, either. It's for anyone – dads, partners or grandparents, whoever's doing the caring – who just wants some fresh ideas to help reduce the time they spend tidying, cleaning and washing so that they can spend more time with children. It applies just as much to the brand new mother who can't find a moment to blow-dry her hair as to the company director who's struggling to get her three kids to school by 9am.

It's also about carving out some more 'me time' – some periods when you can recharge your batteries. There's a good reason they tell you on aeroplanes to put on your own oxygen mask before helping anyone else. It's not just your child who needs sleep, exercise and the chance to let off steam. But without strategies for setting aside those precious hours, many of us are losing out on a vital resource for maintaining our well-being. Unless we reclaim some of that time, we risk losing our connection to ourselves and, beyond that, our connection to our children and our partners.

Some ideas will apply to your life; others won't. Dip in and out and try one or two at a time – and see if they make a difference. You will know instinctively what will work for you and your family. Keep this book in your bag for the 30 seconds you snatch when the baby's asleep in the back of the car – or the 10 minutes when you finally get a seat on the train home from work. If there are some sections that appeal to you more than others, skip straight there.

The reason I wrote this book is because when I brought my first baby, Lily, home I promised her that I would be an amazing mother. But when other pressures started to steal away the hours I always meant to spend with her, I became less and less the parent I wanted to be. So I wrote this book to help myself – and other parents – reclaim that promise.

Kitchen craziness:

save yourself time and stress

Feeding children healthy foods – and then cleaning up afterwards – is probably the single most time-consuming challenge for a parent. But with the right equipment and a bit of forethought, there are a whole host of quick, fuss-free family meals that won't leave your kitchen looking like a bombsite – and will make for more relaxed mealtimes.

Stress-free mealtimes

The key to getting out of the kitchen quicker is to head off disasters before they happen. Imagine how much sooner you would be liberated if you didn't end up on your hands and knees at the end of every meal chipping food off the floor.

The right high chair
If your children are still at the baby and toddler stage, you will save hours of cleaning up simply by choosing the right high chair.

My life changed the day I traded in my quaint little wooden chair for a not-so-pretty plastic version with a huge tray. The difference was that no matter how hard the baby tried to lob her food over the edge, the tray was now wider than her arms could stretch. It also had a raised border to stop food falling off the edge. In fact, the whole kitchen area stayed cleaner because there was now much less food ending up on the floor – and then getting traipsed around.

When picking out a high chair, check that the tray can be removed really easily so you can dump all the debris straight in the bin and give it a quick rinse under the hot tap. When your baby's beginning to master finger foods, that means you will have a fresh, clean, hygienic eating surface every time – with the added bonus of saving you having to wash up dishes and plates which would otherwise also get lobbed off.

Forget beauty here. Look for a design free of nooks and crannies that will trap food and which is easy to wipe down.

If food does get cemented and into all sorts of corners, don't spend hours scrubbing. Instead, take it outside and wash it down with a high-pressure hose.

Floor mats and place mats

How often have you looked under the kitchen table and wondered if anything you prepared actually made it into your children's mouths? When you have young children, the amount of debris can be frightening – and constantly picking it all up is one of those jobs that makes you feel like a drudge.

Make it manageable by investing in a washable plastic mat to go under high chairs and eating areas.

Don't bother with the flimsy bits of tarpaulin you find in baby shops. Instead look for cheaper, harder-wearing mats that you can order in a range of patterns and sizes. Just make sure the mat is heavy enough to stay put (more on suction pads below) but light and easy enough to shake out into the sink – or shove in the washing machine when things get really messy.

Don't stop there. Invest in some plastic table mats to catch the overspill from plates. They just seem to stop the mess spreading all over the table – and again you can quickly rinse them off in the sink. Suction pads (a pack of 20 will cost less than £2 if you can't find ones that come with the suckers) will help keep them stay put – and buying plates and bowls with these will also be a life-saver during the phase when your child thinks plate-throwing is the best fun there is.

As soon as they are out of the high chair, praise kids for sitting square-on at the table, and push their chairs right in. This will also dramatically reduce mess.

The best bib
Buying bibs in the right size, shape and fabric is essential if you want to avoid changing your baby or young toddler after most mealtimes. Make sure one is always handy by fixing a hook on the back of your high chair.

Design-wise, the most useless of all are those tiny little terry towel ones that cover about two inches square. Plus you need to wash them, which only adds to your laundry mountain.

All in all, the wipe-clean plastic-coated ones with a pocket at the bottom to catch the fall-out are generally the most practical. The latest versions come in more rubbery designs, making them easier for your child to wear. They can also be thrown in the dishwasher with the plates.

Disposable bibs are a great thing to keep in your handbag when you are heading out. They take up hardly any room, cut down on laundry and later on you won't find any nasty surprises at the bottom of your bag.

Stress-free cups and glasses

Ever been greeted by an avalanche of plastic sippy cups on opening your cupboard and then found you didn't have a single lid that fitted any of them? As I learned from bitter experience, sippy cups, like bibs, are not an area to economise in.

Find the best make and model – something that is easy to clean and assemble without an instruction manual and promises to be 100% leak-proof for little ones. If you buy the same brand, you will be able to stack them neatly so that they won't cascade out of the cupboard when you open it. Plus you won't be unloading the entire cupboard in an infuriating search for a lid that fits – because all the lids will do the job.

As children get older, they won't want to be seen drinking out of sippy cups, so let them choose some funky sports or hot drinks beakers which come in bright colours. They have covers and won't break. Or to head off spills, cover a beaker with clingfilm and stick a straw through it.

If your child is prone to knocking his cup over at the table, avoid those spills by buying some thick rolls of gaffer tape to use as cup holders.

Easy dishes

Buy plates and bowls in the same shape and size, so they stack easily. Keep them in a pile at the front of the cupboard for easy access. Better still, use shallow bowls, instead of rimless plates, to stop kids pushing the food off and onto the table.

While it's a lovely idea to serve up food in china Bunnykins bowls, most toddlers go through a phase of Greek-style plate-throwing. So get plastic dishes – again with those suction pads – so your child won't be experimenting with gravity at mealtimes. Better still, melamine is more attractive – it looks and feels like china, but is just as durable as plastic.

You don't need to bother with plates or bowls every time either. Serve babies finger foods on their high chair tray and serve older kids snacks on a bread board so they can help themselves.

As far as cutlery goes, opt for cheap and cheerful (the IKEA set comes highly recommended for best value) – because, like socks, spoons and forks tend to disappear.

Your kitchen essentials

Now that you've headed off a host of disasters before they have even happened, here's the basic equipment you need to make your time in the kitchen as stress-free as possible.

A big freezer

Your tissue-box-sized freezer compartment was no doubt fine before you had children – all you needed it for was a half-eaten tub of Ben & Jerry's. But now you have kids, you need something more substantial.

A generous-sized freezer cuts out the dreaded last-minute dash to the shops with little ones in tow. It also means you can cook in bulk, and you can always produce a meal from somewhere, no matter how hectic your day has been. What's more, you won't need to excavate through the ice to get to the fish fingers at the back.

The easiest freezers are the upright style with drawers, so you can 'file' your food in the right compartment – and find what you need quickly. Get Tupperware that fits in your freezer nicely, so you can stack prepared meals without wasting space.

A microwave

A microwave is every parent-in-a-hurry's best friend. Not only because it's quick, but also because it saves on endless washing-up.

Don't you hate those stringy eggy saucepans? With a microwave, all you have to do is crack an egg into a cup and after 55 seconds you've got a perfect poached egg – without the mess.

During the baby stage, microwaved bananas, mixed with warm milk, are easy early food. Also buy some microwave bags to sterilise bottles. As kids get older, you can microwave complete mini meals in a mug, ranging from cheesy nachos to scrambled eggs to mushroom risotto and macaroni cheese. Usually you can just throw all the ingredients in, microwave in a couple of bursts, stir it a few times – and out comes the perfect child-size hot meal before their eyes.

Some easy microwave meals to inspire you . . .

Macaroni cheese. Get a mug, put in a handful of macaroni (you can also use shell-shape pasta) and then fill to just under three-quarters full with water – or milk if you want it more creamy. Then stand your mug in a microwave bowl to catch any liquid that bubbles over. Cover the mug with cling film and pierce with a fork. Microwave on high for two minutes. Pour any water that has overflowed into the bowl back into the mug and stir so the macaroni does not stick at the bottom, and cook for a further two minutes. Add some cheese and butter – which should now melt in – and stir so it coats the macaroni. If you want it a little more melted, put back in the microwave for another 20 seconds. To make it more substantial, throw in some veg such as sweetcorn. You can also jazz it up by using up leftover bits of cheese from the fridge.

Banana breakfast bread. Mix three tablespoons of self-raising flour with three tablespoons of sugar and a beaten egg in your mug. Then add a drop or two of vanilla essence with a tablespoon each of oil and milk, together with a mashed ripe banana. For extra flavour, you can add in a sprinkle of cinnamon or some extra protein in the form of a few walnuts or pecans. Mix well, put in the microwave on high and check every minute or so for up to three minutes until it's cooked through but still nice and moist.

YouTube has lots of demonstrations showing you how to make all sorts of mug recipes, from blueberry muffins to quiche, in less than five minutes.

Just make sure you give everything you make standing time to cool down once it's removed from the microwave – the insides can be very hot. Also make holes if the container needs clingfilm, so that steam doesn't build up and burst out when you peel it off.

The perfect kitchen bin
The best test of a parent-friendly item is whether you can use it with one hand. So look for bins with one-touch flip-top lids, or a foot pedal, because they are a dream to use even with a child on your arm.

Look for a good-quality model with a generous capacity – 50 litres should do the trick – so you are not emptying it every five minutes. Also check that it has a strong inner ring which holds securely to your black rubbish bag. Fishing it out when it has dropped to the bottom – and after all the rubbish has tipped out – is one of the world's most unpleasant jobs.

The right size dishwasher
They may all look pretty similar, but not all dishwashers are alike, and this is not an item to scrimp on. Get a large-capacity one. A full dishwasher can be a serious blockage in a chaotic kitchen and you want to be unloading it as seldom as possible. Save yourself having to traipse all over the kitchen to unload, by using the cupboards nearest your machine to store your cutlery, saucepans and crockery. Employ your model to full advantage by washing more than pots and pans: a dishwasher can also save you time by cleaning dust pans, gummed-up soap dishes, toothbrush holders, fridge shelves, vacuum cleaner attachments and plastic wastebins.

An easy blender
You don't want to be messing about with lots of blades and attachments, so buy the simplest model. You can't go wrong with the jug-style type for making everything from puréed baby food to smoothies and – when the kids have gone to bed – cocktails.

Don't worry about washing the jug. Let it clean itself by filling up the jug with warm water and washing liquid and switching it on high for 30 seconds.

Children love experimenting with smoothie combinations – and it's quite simply the easiest and most entertaining way of getting vitamins into children ever invented.

The right mops
When you are cleaning up after children, choosing the right mop and floor-cleaner will save you an obscene amount of time.

Don't skimp. Invest in two different types.

- First, a shaggy dust mop with the widest head possible – the industrial type office cleaners use. It means you can push all the food debris into one place with just a couple of sweeps of the room. It should also have a swivelling head, so you can sweep up all the crumbs and food bits which have gathered around the edges.
- Second, forget squeegee mops or string mops and buckets. Far too much work. They leave the floor awash, and need constant wringing out. Instead use a microfibre mop. They can absorb up to seven times their own weight in fluid, and attract dust naturally, so you don't have to use chemicals.

Then the only other thing you need is a spray bottle. Mix a strong cleaning solution with water. Keep it handy and spray sparingly, and then run the microfibre mop over the floor. When the mop head gets dirty, just detach it and throw it in the washing machine. It will more than halve the time you spend cleaning the floor – and your chaotic kitchen will feel under control.

A kitchen blackboard
A big blackboard in your kitchen is an invaluable way of keeping everyone on message. Make it big enough for everyone in the family to be able to reach it and write on it. Turn it into the organisational hub by keeping ongoing shopping and to-do lists, a large calendar, as well as your household rules (more on that later) – and the children's weekly activity schedules.

The one I have in my kitchen is three feet long, made out of plywood covered with blackboard paint, and it even has a section for my younger daughter's weekly spellings. Make your own at very little cost with magnetic blackboard paint so you can stick up school notices too. Or paint it straight onto the wall.

As kids get older, make them share responsibility for keeping it up to date. So whoever uses the last spoonful of mayonnaise also has the job of adding it to the shopping list.

A good old-fashioned pantry
Avoid last-minute panics for essential staples by finding some cupboard space somewhere in your home to use as a 'pantry'.

If you don't have the space, it doesn't have to be in the kitchen – it just has to be a cool place to store the things everyone runs out of, like toilet paper, juice cartons, paper towels, washing powder, soap, cereal and canned foods. If you can keep it organised with a different shelf for each category, all the better.

If you are feeling super-organised when you are unpacking your groceries, stack cans and soups of the same type on top of one another with the labels facing outwards. That way you can see how many you have and what you are running low on.

Equipment essentials

A well-designed toaster. A toaster is key to the smooth running of your breakfast time, so choose carefully. Look for a more expensive one with an easily removable tray so that it doesn't spew a never-ending fountain of breadcrumbs over your countertops. Or simply place a tray underneath as a guaranteed catch-all. Before you buy, check that the toast pops right up, rather than tempting you to singe your fingers or, worse still, use a fork to fish it out. Wooden tongs – which are as little as £1 each to buy – will also help get your toast out of a tight spot if you're in a rush. Look for a toaster with slots wide enough to take crumpets, buns and bagels to avoid the bother of using your oven grill.

Sharp knives. Nothing is more frustrating or time-wasting than a blunt one – and have a good sharpener on hand to keep the ones you have working well.

A pair of kitchen scissors. Absolutely the quickest way to cut up ham and countless other types of meat – and once you've used it to slice up pizza, you'll never use one of those rolling pizza slicers again. Have them on hand to cut up herbs, slice the stems off flowers and open packaging...

A quality tin-opener. As much as I wish they did, not all tins come with handy ring-pulls. Tin-openers do wear out, and if you're struggling to open a tin for a second longer than you need to, nothing will rescue it. So bin it and get a new one that does the job smoothly.

An easy-to-use kitchen timer. When you've got demanding children in the background, it's easy to take your eye off the ball – and boiling pan – with messy consequences.

A decent spatula. Save your fingers, and stop trying to dangle hot food precariously from forks, and invest in a couple of good-sized spatulas for lifting fish fingers, burgers, sausages and pizza. Or use silicone tongs.

Good saucepans. Better-quality pans will cook more evenly and are less likely to scorch food. Get them with lids so they heat food faster and more economically when needed. Make sure they have heat-resistant handles so they can go in the oven – and so you don't need to find an oven glove to take them off the stove. Even better, get nice-looking large ones so you can save yourself a step and transfer them straight from the oven to the table. Get some cheap ceramic tiles if you need to protect table tops.

Platters, serving plates and jugs. Big platters are for finger foods and family sharing and their large surface means less fetching and carrying for you. Fill a large jug at the start of every meal so you are not running to and fro organising drinks.

Not essential – but nice to have . . .

A clingfilm dispenser. Get one if you want to save yourself the frustration of searching for the edge. It also enables you to tear off the right amount straight away.

A grater – with a box attachment. This saves time by catching the cheese so it's ready to use. Remember, a good grater can also save you minutes when you're shredding hard veg like cabbage, carrots, onions, potatoes and cucumber, as well as garlic or chocolate.

A mandolin. One step up from a grater, this is a sort of sloping blade. When you pass fruit and vegetables along it in a sawing motion, it is simply the most efficient way to slice them. Each piece will also come out the same thickness so everything will cook evenly. With one of these acting like a sous-chef, you can have the ingredients for a stir-fry ready in a minute or less. Tomatoes and potatoes are also dealt with in moments, as well as apples and oranges. Just don't think of buying one without a hand guard as these things are sharp.

A pizza tray. These come with a mesh-like base, so the heat transfers more easily through the bottom, cooks the pizza quicker and gives you a crisper crust.

Toaster bags. These re-usable bags cost next to nothing, prevent crumbs falling into the toaster and allow you to make toasted sandwiches, which are ready to take with you if you are rushing out of the house.

A dishwasher-safe mesh bag. Again very cheap, this is also a great item to have on hand. Put in all the fiddly bits that would otherwise get lost in the machine – or take ages to collect – like mixer parts, chopsticks or lots of different pastry cutters after the kids have finished baking.

An all-in-one breakfast pan. Lakeland is now selling a frying pan with different compartments for each item in a full English breakfast. Not cheap at £59.99, but definitely a way of minimising the hassle and washing-up.

Key food items

Your food cupboard

Here are a few things that won't go off quickly – and can get you out of a tight spot if you are running low on supplies.

Powdered cheese. Lasts practically forever – and though you may not win any accolades from Gordon Ramsay, grated Parmesan-style cheese is good to have in the cupboard to add excitement to soups and pastas.

Coconut sprinkles. Like a healthy version of hundreds and thousands, these can make a so-so dessert, like Greek yoghurt, seem exciting if you scatter them on top. Plus it's a sneaky way to get more fruit into kids.

Whipped cream in a can. It can be put on top of any dessert – and then sprinkled with coconut or chocolate milk powder to make any pudding look like a treat – for example, bananas, tinned peaches and pineapple.

Frozen yoghurt lollies. If you put anything on the end of a stick, children love it. So frozen yoghurt or smoothie lollies make a great treat – and kids don't even realise they are good for them. Admittedly they are messy for younger kids, so get them to eat them over a bowl – or slot a cupcake case onto the lolly stick to catch the drips.

Eggs. They last safely for weeks in the fridge, and you will always be able to cook up a quick omelette or scrambled eggs.

Different types of milk. Long life milk is not ideal, but it's worth having a couple of cartons for those mornings when you suddenly realise you've run dry. Other types of milk, like almond and rice milk, also store well and are good for smoothies and porridge where kids may not spot the difference.

Rice and pasta. Without doubt, the core of a kid-friendly kitchen. Give them wholewheat versions, which have a lower glycaemic index and will keep them fuller for longer. After dinner they won't be so hyper, will settle more easily at bedtime – and won't wake up in the middle of the night feeling hungry. Until they are old enough, choose pasta twists and tubes over spaghetti to make it easier to eat. Admittedly, grains of rice can spill everywhere and can be a nightmare to pick up afterwards. So try rice pasta, which cooks in eight minutes, looks just the same as regular pasta, and doesn't make such a mess.

Noodles. Also for a change, try noodles. Just stir with soy sauce, sweetcorn and peas.

Couscous. This is so easy that when I first tried it I thought there must be a catch. But no. Simply pour some boiling water over some couscous and leave for around five minutes until it's all absorbed. Then fluff it up with a fork and add butter or vegetables, like sweetcorn or chickpeas.

Juice cartons. Cartons of concentrated juice often have long expiration dates and are cheaper and easy to buy in bulk because they don't need to be stored in the fridge. They are also useful for smoothies. The sugar content is higher than regular juice, so use sparingly and dilute with water.

Pesto. A versatile ingredient to keep in the fridge which can be used to make lots of staples interesting, ranging from pasta and rice to couscous, or as a tasty crust on fish or meat. It does have quite a high salt content, so don't overdo it.

Terrific tins

In our obsession with 'fresh' and 'organic', tinned food has long been the poor relation, considered only good for baked beans and tomato soup when the cupboard is bare. But just because canned goods are cheap and convenient it doesn't mean they're unhealthy.

It's likely that since the last time you looked, food manufacturers have moved with the times. Most have cut down on sugar and salt, and now pack fruit in its own juice, instead of sickly syrups.

I know I sound like a bit of a convert, but the fact is that, as food prices continue to rise and we have less time to shop for fresh food, tinned food can be a life-saver. Did you know that tinned fruit and vegetables often contain *more* nutrients because the contents are canned when the flavour, minerals and vitamins are at their height? Compare that to fresh fruit and veg which can lose up to 50% of its vitamins in the first seven days after picking.[13] There are fewer preservatives needed too.

Busy parents can be wary about cooking fresh fish – despite how important it is for brain development. After all, it's got a short shelf life, is pretty expensive, can be fiddly to prepare – and after all that, picky children often refuse to eat it.

So in my book, the tinned versions win every time for ease as well as price. They're ready to use straight from the cupboard – and around half the cost. Be subtle, if you have to, and stir tuna into pasta sauces or use it as a sandwich filling.

Tinned fruit and veg is also a godsend – and tinned carrots and potatoes have come a long way since the days when they tasted like war rations. Now that fruit is canned in pure juice, you can empty a tin of pineapples, peaches and strawberries into a bowl and have a ready-made fruit salad in less than a minute – with virtually no chopping or peeling. Canned kidney and chickpeas are also a fantastic source of low-cost, good quality protein. You can use them straight from the tin (after draining) in salads, stews and curries – and they don't need soaking.

Tinned goods to keep in your larder

Apricots and peaches (in juice, not syrup)

Pineapple

Artichoke hearts

Chopped tomatoes

Sweetcorn

Chickpeas and kidney beans

Baked beans (reduced sugar and salt version)

Tomato soup

Pilchards and sardines

Salmon

Tuna (not in brine – to lower salt content)

Freezer items

Frozen fruit. It's frozen at its freshest, won't spoil, will keep for ages and there are lots of different uses for it. Just like ice lollies, my kids love frozen fruit straight from the freezer. Blueberries, strawberries, and grapes chopped in half (so they are not a choking hazard) are always big favourites. They can also be mixed into quick ice-cold smoothies, and make porridge more fun.

If your bananas are going black, don't throw them out. Freeze them so they can be kept to add to milk for banana smoothies (add oats, nuts or seeds for a quick child-friendly breakfast choice) or to use in banana muffins.

Protein staples. Frozen chicken, burgers, salmon and cod are easy to cook and usually go down well with kids. With a microwave, they will only take a few minutes to thaw. Make them more exciting – and quicker to cook – by cutting them up and putting them on a stick with some chopped grilled vegetables for kebabs.

Bread and milk. Keep bread in the freezer and it won't go mouldy. Take out slice by slice for perfect toast in the morning – and let milk defrost in the fridge. Save your crusts and keep in a freezer bag to use as a crunchy topping for macaroni cheese or shepherd's pie.

Fresh vegetables. We all know the feeling of pulling out handfuls of wilted, forgotten vegetables from the bottom of the fridge. So look to your freezer: veg have usually been frozen very quickly after harvesting, and often contain even more vitamins than the fresh stuff, whose nutrient content will have depleted. Beans, broccoli and peas are all often easier to use frozen than tinned. Edamame – soya beans that children can pop out of the shell like jumping beans – are often a huge hit even with the fussiest veggie-hating children – and frozen is the best way to buy those too.

Baby foods. Of course, you already know that you can freeze a month's baby food at a time. Infants starting solids don't need much to begin with, so freeze in ice-cube trays. Then empty into a bag – but label as clearly as possible. If you have older kids as well as a baby, relax a little. Instead just do a mushed-up salt-free baby version of whatever your older children eat.

Speed it up: how to get out of the kitchen quicker

Plan your meals

At the end of a long day, most of us haven't got a lot of mental energy left over to deal creatively with the 'what to fix for dinner' problem. So draw up a meal plan for the month ahead, full of easy main courses that you know your kids like. Consult everyone and have fun by pretending you are drawing up a restaurant menu, or write up this week's menu on your kitchen blackboard. It might take half an hour, but stick to it over the next few months – or until boredom creeps in – and you will be surprised by how much more in control you feel.

Or if you want to make it really, really simple, do the same meal on each day of the week – and you can even name them memorably with names like Taco Tuesdays or Fish Fridays, so you don't forget. That's still enough variety for most children. Plus kids love routine and knowing what's coming next. Everyone's on the same page and there won't be so much debate, because it's all been agreed up front.

Save the simplest supper for nights you know will be hectic. There's something oddly comforting about a quick plate of poached eggs every Sunday evening when there's homework to be done and school bags to be packed.

So now you've decided what to cook, here are lots of ways of making the cooking process even quicker.

Quick cooking

- While you're cooking, put a container on the countertop to hold all your peelings, packaging and waste. That way the counter will look under control and you won't be running back and forward to the dustbin.
- If you're adding vegetables to pasta, chuck them into the same saucepan for the last four minutes to save on washing up.
- When you're cooking pasta or vegetables, boil the water
- in a kettle first – it's faster and more energy efficient.
- Make a hole in the middle of hamburgers. They cook faster – and the holes close up by the time they're ready.
- Grill rather than bake. It's faster. Salmon steaks and sausages, which take up to 20 minutes to bake, can be grilled in less than half the time because the heat is so much more concentrated.
- If you haven't got a microwave, cook baked potatoes more quickly by pushing a metal skewer through each one.
- To cook chicken in roughly half the time, pound it flat. Cut large cuts of meat in two.

- Use foil when you're grilling. No parent wants to spend precious time scrubbing off caked-on grease. In fact, never underestimate the power of aluminium foil. You can line any dish and you won't have the chore of scrubbing them afterwards. Non-stick parchment will also spare you greasy clean-ups.
- When you are making cakes or pastry, put sheets of newspaper over the countertops to catch all the floury mess. Instead of wiping down afterwards, just scrunch up the newspapers and throw them away. If you are making cookies, keep some extra dough and freeze it so you have some handy next time the children want to bake and you haven't got time to start from scratch.
- Make big batches of staple meals on Sunday. Then reheat them during the week. Freeze the complete meal, not just the sauce.
- If you're making loads of soup, reduce any leftovers for freezing so that it takes up less room in the freezer. You can dilute the soup again when you reheat it.

To really simplify ... try recipes that use four ingredients or fewer

Foodies might see it as sacrilege, but if you really want to simplify your cooking, there are a range of cookbooks and recipes on the internet for main meals made with no more than four ingredients. One of my personal favourite books is aptly called *4 Ingredients* (published by Four Ingredients, 2008) and each of the 340 recipes is no more than four lines long, with no weighing or measuring, so you really can make them while you're half-distracted by children. You might not win any gastronomy prizes, but pesto chicken (chicken breast halves, one tablespoon of olive oil, three tablespoons of basil pesto and some mozzarella slices) or mushroom risotto (mushrooms, Arborio rice, vegetable stock and Parmesan) really is fresh cooking you can do when you're under the cosh.

Let them help themselves

Children don't always need to be served perfectly prepared food. For them, much of the joy of eating comes from feeling the texture of food and trying different tastes, rather than always being presented with a complete meal they feel they have to eat up. Try giving them some of the raw materials and let them do more of the assembly themselves. Self-serve meals are often fun as well as being surprisingly easy for parents too.

Pizza. Once a week, give them a pizza base, chop up the raw ingredients, grate some cheese and get them to build their own pizzas.

Mexican wraps or taco shells. Stuff a tortilla wrap or taco shell with beans mixed with a ready-made Mexican sauce and then let kids build their own by adding sliced lettuce, diced tomatoes, sour cream, avocado and topping it off with grated cheese.

Cheese on toast. It's simple to make, so let kids jazz it up with different coloured cheeses – try red Leicester for example – and experiment with condiments.

Baked potatoes. Bake a selection of smaller ones and let kids choose what to stuff them with, ranging from tuna and sweetcorn to different kinds of gooey cheese, like Brie.

Kitchen organisation tricks

- When you've got a lot going on, it's easy to forget even the tastiest recipe. So stick the ingredients and directions of your favourite standbys inside your kitchen cabinets, use Post-it notes to mark them in your cookery books, or bookmark them on your phone.
- Keep your tools under control. Are your dessert spoons impossible to get to under a tangle of whisks and garlic crushers? Keep the stuff you need most often in a jug next to the cooker so you can see what you need and grab it right away instead of rifling through drawers. What's more, why lay the table every night when you can stick a week's worth of cutlery in the middle of the table in a glass jar for everyone to take their own?
- Use larger mixing bowls than you think you'll need so whatever you are blending doesn't splash or overflow. This also means that you won't need to pour the mix into a larger bowl halfway through the preparation.
- Keep a sink filled with hot soapy water to rinse utensils and soak pots as you go. It's especially important with breakfast bowls that are spattered with cereal – or, worst of all, porridge. Left out all day, they can harden to the consistency of concrete.
- Try to wipe spills off the hob as soon as they happen – before they dry rock hard. To stop spilled food making black marks, pour salt on the spillage.
- Take two minutes to throw out any old food and give the fridge a wipe just before you put your new shopping in. Throw away whatever has been lurking at the back of the freezer since you bought it. After two years, I guarantee you will never, ever feel like eating it. Move food with pending expiration dates to the front so it doesn't get forgotten.

- Only stock your fridge with nutritious snacks that you are happy for your older children to eat. Keep them at their level at the front, so they can help themselves – with your permission.
- Clear out any clutter that has nothing to do with cooking. Make the most of your worktop space by keeping out only appliances you use every day. Toasters and microwaves are useful. Giant juicers, which only get used twice a year on the first day of your health kick, are not. Where possible, also use wall space to get things off the surfaces by buying magnetic knife holders and hanging spice racks.
- Appalled by the amount of grease that builds up on the tops of your kitchen cupboards and your fridge? Head off the heinous job of wiping it off by cutting greaseproof paper to size and putting it on top. Then, rather than have to swab off all the muck yourself, remove and replace the paper.
- In the summer, reduce your floor and surface cleaning time and have more fun by suggesting the kids have a picnic outside.
- Cook meals for the children – like chillies or casseroles – that with a bit of spicing up can double as meals for you and your partner when the children are in bed, if you are not all eating together. Stock your cupboard with ingredients like mustard, oils, dried herbs, soy sauce, spices and herb pastes so that you can transform a kid's meal into a more adult dinner.

Five-minute meals

Pitta bread pizza. Don't faff about waiting for the pizza dough to cook. Instead, pop a piece of pitta bread in the toaster to warm both sides, and while it's doing that, turn the grill on. Then cover one side with tomato paste, cheese and then other toppings like tuna, mushrooms or sausage – and heat.

Scrambled egg and smoked salmon. With omega 3-packed quality protein, and served with wholemeal bread, this is pretty much the perfect meal – in about five minutes.

Chops and sausages. Just grill in minutes (with some foil at the bottom of the tray) for the feeling you are giving your kids a real meat supper.

Soup with wholemeal toast. Don't feel guilty about serving soup. It can be a power food and there are lots of ways to make sure it's packed with protein. Pea and ham soup, lentil soup and chowders are all great meals in themselves. Even a bog-standard can of Heinz cream of tomato soup, at 84% tomatoes, is one of your five a day and can become an even more complete meal with some grated Cheddar cheese on top and served with some brown bread and butter soldiers.

Cod and veg. Chuck a piece of cod (or better still a more sustainable fish) in a saucepan with some frozen peas and carrots, some milk and butter – and you have a creamy wholesome meal.

Roast chicken drumsticks. Cheat by buying roast chicken drumsticks and then pop them under the grill to make them tender and sizzling, as if you'd cooked them from scratch yourself.

Pasta with cheesy tomato sauce and veg. Throw in frozen broccoli and sweetcorn with the pasta. Then drain and stir in some tomato paste and Cheddar cheese to make it gooey – and it's done. Another variation is to stir in cream cheese with ham or smoked salmon for protein.

Breakfast for dinner

On occasional evenings when you are late home or the kids are tired, you won't kill them by giving them a bowl of cereal or, better still, porridge. These days most cereals are nutritionally fortified – and don't forget that muesli was originally designed as a nutritionally perfect food. Buy the bite-size versions and the brands without sugar. Granted, it may sound a bit Victorian, but porridge is quick and can easily be turned into a nutritious meal by adding fruit, seeds and nuts.

Pimp your porridge
Many children love porridge. Like any staple it can get boring, but there are ways to vary a bowl so the kids keep coming back for more.

- Peanut butter is a children's favourite. It's packed full of protein and tastes great in porridge. Add a dollop as you're heating up the oats and milk, followed by maple syrup or honey at the end. This also works with Nutella. Pop on some sliced banana as a garnish.
- Spice it up with cinnamon. If you're having a lazier day, try heating some chopped apple and raisins for five minutes and then mixing this into the porridge with a teaspoon of cinnamon powder.
- Add some Greek yoghurt, runny honey, and serve with some flaked almonds on top.

Cheese

Cheese is a high-protein, versatile food that's good for filling children up – and adding calcium to their diets with minimum effort. But don't just stick to Cheddar. If you start them young, they will be soon ready to entertain a whole range of varieties.

Halloumi. Its robust texture makes this cheese wonderfully grillable. Slice it into strips and cook for five minutes for easy finger food. It is high in salt, though, so look for lower-salt varieties, or only make it as an occasional snack.

Goats' cheese and ricotta Start kids early enough and they will love its creamy consistency. It also works well with fruit, like pears.

Mozzarella. The ultimate fun cheese that children love because it's so stringy when it melts, and it's fun to eat on the top of pizzas and in baked potatoes. It also makes a super-quick salad added to slices of tomatoes or avocado – and has one of the lowest salt contents of any cheese.

Swiss cheese. Often comes in slices, so it's incredibly easy to slip into sandwiches and also very easy to roll with other sliced foods, such as chicken, as an alternative to sarnies in lunchboxes.

Brie and Camembert. Wonderfully gooey; Camembert can be a lovely snack lunch if you bake it in the oven.

Healthy no-cook meals

For some reason, many of us feel we are not being good parents if we aren't preparing our children a hot meal every day. While there is something comforting about that idea, let yourself off the hook. Food that's raw often has more nutrients and can be just as satisfying – and even more varied than cooked food. So try these ideas:

Children's ploughman's. This is fun for your kids to eat, and there's no washing up afterwards. Try oatcakes, hummus, cold chicken drumsticks and halved baby tomatoes. Just make sure there's a good selection of protein, wholegrain carbs and vegetables.

Crunchy raw vegetables. Don't feel you always have to cook veg. Children often actually prefer something to crunch. As a side order at meals, present them with manageable little ramekin dishes of carrot sticks, crisp runner beans, sliced multi-coloured peppers or mini tomatoes.

Kebabs. Kids love anything on a stick. Halve cherry tomatoes and alternate with little rounds of mozzarella. You can also try this with fruit – cubes of melon and kiwi look gorgeous. In fact, if you cut anything into regular bite-size pieces and arrange them in some sort of order, they look more appetising. Take the points off the skewers, though.

One-pot cooking

A healthy home-cooked family meal doesn't have to use every piece of cookware in your kitchen – or take hours to clean up afterwards. For larger family dinners, go for one-pot recipes, putting all the ingredients into a single dish and letting them cook together.

Better still, invest in a slow cooker or 'crock pot'. They are electrically powered to cook at low temperatures over longer periods. That way you could throw a few things in the pot while you're making breakfast in the morning, leave it with no risk of burning, and have a hot meal ready for supper when you come home. They are especially good for casseroles, curries and chillies and any dishes containing meat like chicken and lamb.

For example, try pouring a tin of mushroom soup over chicken thighs with carrots and potatoes in the morning and leaving it on a low heat. You won't even have to look at it again until it's ready to dish up. Plus there's barely any washing up.

Helping kids to eat fruit and veg without a row

When you are a parent, no one looks forward to time-consuming power struggles – they're no fun for anyone. But what happens when the issue is something as important as eating fruit and veg – and your children point blank refuse to eat their five a day? Here are some quick and easy ways of making sure kids get their full complement of fruit and veg – without them even realising it.

Dip them. Make it fun by giving them dips to dunk their veggies in. Try hummus, soft cheese, yoghurt dips or guacamole. They'll be more interested in dipping than the fact that they are eating something that's good for them.

Spread them. Try nut butters instead of butter or margarine to get more good fats into your child's diet. As well as peanut butter, you could also try hazelnut and cashew nut versions.

Mini-size them. Adult-sized portions of fruit and veg can put small children off. So choose small fruit and veg, like baby plum tomatoes, baby sweetcorn and mini carrots. They will also find two or three smaller baked potatoes more fun to put fillings and toppings on (melted cheese or tuna, for example) than one huge one. 'Fun-size' apples, which are about 20% smaller than normal ones, are less daunting and better suited to a child's appetite, as well as saving you time chopping and tidying. They will also spare you the frustration of seeing kids taking one bite and leaving the rest.

Pop them. Let your children pop the beans out of edamame or the peas out of pea pods. The end result will be too tempting to resist.

Blend them. Make soups by steaming lots of vegetables until soft, then add boiling water and blend into a smooth soup with a hand blender. Broccoli, cauliflower, carrots, parsnips, swedes, spinach, tomatoes, squash, sweet potatoes and celery can all be thrown in – and by the time it's come out of the mixer, kids won't have a clue what went into it. All they'll know is that it's a cool colour.

Experiment with smoothies. Kids love throwing different types of fruit in the blender, pressing the button and seeing what shade the smoothie comes out. Try bananas, mangoes, pineapples, papayas, peaches, nectarines, pears and all the different berries. Even slip some kale in there. With the stronger tasting fruit, they won't notice it. Smoothies also make the perfect fast breakfast for you and the children. Throw in a banana, milk, nuts and oats for a filling and nutritious start to the day.

Compartmentalise. For younger children, use an ice-cube tray and put bite-size portions of colourful fruit and veg in each compartment. If you feel your kids aren't eating enough good foods at main meals, let them snack from it all day if they want to. They're more likely to eat from it because it feels like their idea.

How to deal with time-consuming picky eating

Many parents get stressed about picky eating, but trying to force children to eat can unwittingly make the issue worse – and create more resistance. At mealtimes, anything your child wants to eat is going to be gobbled up in the first 15 minutes. After that, they've probably lost interest and you're wasting your time. Pushing a loaded spoonful of food into a child's face will just put them off even more, and will turn mealtimes into a power struggle.

Let them help. As you cook, get kids feeling curious and involved by offering them a little taste. Let them add ingredients and stir as you go along. It will feel like more fun and they may be more open to trying some of the finished product on their plates.

Offer limited choices. Help children feel they have a say by involving them in decisions, albeit limited ones, like 'Would you like broad beans or sweetcorn with your fish?' Afterwards praise them for making a good decision.

Serve littler portions. Kids can find it off-putting to be faced with mountains of food. Give smaller, more tantalising portions so they are more likely to finish and ask for more.

Make it look fun. It's astonishing how easily you can make a food child-friendly by cutting shapes out of it with a biscuit cutter. In a flash, cucumber and melon slices are transformed into stars or dinosaurs.

Keep offering new things. Just because kids say 'Yuck' when they try something new doesn't mean you should stop trying. Give them lots of chances to try foods you are eating – as their tastes will develop as they get older. Remember that it can take children up to 15 tries before they get used to a new flavour. Let them try eating straight off your plate. The more they eat what you eat, the easier it will be in the long run.

Try food bridges. If you know they like passion fruit, try them on kiwis next. If they have developed a taste for peas, move onto broad beans.

Don't cajole with puddings. Who hasn't told a child to eat their main course if they want pudding? Bribes work at first – so it may look like you have cracked it when they hoover up what's on their plate to get their afters. But it also sends the message that the main course is the obstacle they have to get around before they get what they really want – a sugary dessert.

Respect some differences. Bear in mind the fact your children will have definite likes and dislikes. Indeed, there are genuine genetic differences behind why kids taste food differently. My younger child would eat broccoli for Britain. My eldest physically gags at the taste of it, but she can't eat enough blueberries and strawberries – so it all evens out.

Don't order children to eat up. In their desperation to get kids to eat healthily, many parents end up trotting out phrases like 'How do you know you don't like it if you haven't even tried it?' or 'Just eat it.' But confrontation will just make a child more anxious and resistant about food. Don't force, cajole, nag or demonise. You will be giving food far too much power if you do. Your child will always win in the short term because at the end of the day, it's their mouth – and they know very well that it's ultimately up to them whether they open it or not. Remember that a healthy child will never starve.

Allow treats. Even if you try to keep sweet things out of your children's way, they will still find out about them and want them more. Don't make them forbidden. There are lots of healthier recipes for cakes and biscuits these days. For example, you could cook your own popcorn – which is cheap, easy and a great source of fibre and antioxidants – and let kids have fun making lots of combinations of flavourings using ingredients like cinnamon and honey.

The benefits of eating together

Parents often use children's mealtimes as a chance to catch up with jobs like putting a wash on. So perhaps it's not surprising that kids try to get your attention by not eating what they are given. Children don't want to sit on their own. So, even if it's only for 10 minutes, take the time to sit down and eat with your child, and set a good example. Even better, wherever possible organise dinner time so that the whole family sits down together.

There are other significant benefits to these meals. On a regular basis, it not only bonds parents and children, it is also one of the single biggest predictors of success for youngsters. Children who eat four meals a week with their families have been shown to do better at school and have fewer conflicts with their parents.

A recent study published in the *Journal of Adolescent Health* found that as children grow up, family meals have a calming effect – and every meal kids regularly have with their family leads to an improvement. It found they feel more included and valued, even if they do not say much at the table, because they are able to see the communication between other members of the family and feel that they are an important part of the unit.[14]

It does not have to be just dinner. Weekend brunches or breakfasts will work just as well.

Make the rules only that you will turn off the TV, put away your phones (try introducing a basket into which all go automatically before the meal starts) and steer clear of parental pep talks.

And you will probably find that your child eats better, too.

Fast lunch boxes

If your child's school has school meals, grab them with both hands. However, there are parents who have no choice, and for them, making up a school lunch box is a nightly chore or morning slog.

The ideal packed lunch should contain protein, whole grains, dairy products, fruit and vegetables. A tall order – but with a few shortcuts, it can be done in a matter of minutes.

- Freeze sandwiches in bulk. Make and cut up a whole loaf and put each round of sandwiches in a freezer bag. Take them out in the morning. They will have defrosted by lunchtime. The same can be done with muffins.

- Cut down the time you spend buttering and slicing bread. Use rolls instead or buy tortillas – fill them with tuna or salad and seal the edges with cream cheese to help them stick.
- If you find your child keeps leaving their apple – and so is not getting their fruit at lunchtime – slice it up. To stop it turning brown in the lunchbox, hold it together by putting a rubber band around it so they can eat it bit by bit like a chocolate orange.
- Use pitta pockets. Just cut off a small hole and stuff with your child's favourite things, like tuna or chicken.
- Leave out the bread element completely. Instead use a thin deli slice of ham or turkey on top of a slice of cheese and roll them up. Cut in half and wrap in foil. Or try it with a slice of salami spread with cream cheese.
- Stick in a piece of pitta bread for your child to tear up and dip into mini pots of hummus.
- Use Tupperware with different compartments, to save having to find lots of little boxes for the different elements.
- Freeze cartons of drinks overnight to act like ice packs to keep food cool and appetising.
- Boil some extra pasta at dinnertime. Stir in pesto and sweetcorn with the leftovers, and store in a Tupperware box for lunch for the next day.
- Use the leftovers from dinner the night before – or even from breakfast. Cold pizza is delicious as an occasional treat, and no less nutritious than a sandwich, if more fat-laden. Fold over into pockets, cut off the crusts, and toast in a toasty bag to turn them into an instant sandwich. Sausages – including the vegetarian kind – are probably tastier cold. Mini pancakes that don't get eaten at breakfast can be surprisingly good – filled with banana slices or strawberries – as a dessert at lunch.

- From the age of eight, make preparing packed lunch your child's responsibility. Try it just two or three days a week at first so it feels like a treat.
- Ask them to do it while you make the supper, so all the mess is over and done with in one go. Lay out the breakfast bowls and cups at the same time.

When you can't face cooking ...

If you choose carefully, take-aways don't have to be unhealthy. For the occasional nights when you just don't have the time, let alone the energy, to cook, keep the menus in your kitchen or office drawer as special treat for you and the kids when you get home.

Fish and chips. Make sure children don't just gorge themselves on the batter and do eat the flesh too. When it comes to chips, the thicker the better – they absorb less fat. Go easy on the salt and include a portion of baked beans to add some veg content.

Italian. When it comes to pizza, stay away from higher-fat cheese-filled crusts and pepperoni and garlic bread. Instead pile on the tomatoes, mushroom, sweetcorn and olives and take advantage of the salad side dishes that are on offer. Rather than just plain pasta, order ravioli filled with vegetables.

Indian. The good news is that Indian food is packed full of vegetables. Just choose the milder, lower-fat options cooked in tomato-based sauces – the tandoori dishes rather than the creamier kormas and pasandas. Watch the deep-fried samosas and pakoras and order veggie and lentil side dishes instead.

Chinese. Opt for stir-fried and steamed, and avoid anything with the word 'crispy' in the title. Choose boiled and egg-fried instead of deep-fried rice. Kids may love them, but don't let them fill up completely on prawn crackers. A healthier option would be Thai food, which is more likely to include steamed rice, fish and veg. And if you can get your children to develop a taste for it, try sushi. Unlikely though it may sound, some children fall in love with the bite-size bundles of flavours, chopsticks and presentation trays – if you offer it without a fuss early enough. If you are worried about the raw fish, choose the veggie kind.

Supermarket shopping

Make your life easier: shop at home

Why anyone would voluntarily brave the supermarket with children in tow is a mystery to me. With younger kids, it feels like a bad version of *Supermarket Sweep* – only with a grenade ticking away in the seat of your trolley. Temptation everywhere – and an audience of hundreds if a tantrum blows up. Avoid where possible, and make the internet delivery services work for you.

- Shop around for the fastest and easiest supermarket site. Make sure they give tight delivery slots so you aren't left hanging around with impatient kids waiting for the shopping to show up. Smaller companies, like Abel & Cole, will also take the stress out of having to be there for the delivery by leaving your order outside your home (in a discreet place) whether you are in or not. You can also set up your order to include the same basic supplies every week, with some items scheduled for once a fortnight or even monthly, so you can always count on getting some supplies even if you completely forget to log on and re-order.

- Consider choosing one of the late-night delivery time slots so you can give your fridge a wipe and unpack the groceries when the children are in bed.
- Keep an ongoing grocery list on your phone or the supermarket's app, so you don't waste time reaching back into the inner recesses of your brain to remember what you need.
- Check the supplier's delivery policy. Pick a company that will bring your food slap-bang into your kitchen. Not, as has happened to me, send a delivery man who refused to cross the threshold, citing health and safety. He then dumped 15 bags on the doorstep for me to haul in with a hysterical baby in my arms. The kitchen was four foot in front of him. Not surprisingly, I switched to a company with a policy of bringing the goods into the kitchen.
- Involve the kids. If your children won't give you a minute to get to the computer, let them help. Now that websites have little pictures of the foods on offer, it can be fun – and even educational for a child learning fruit and veg names, or the meaning of pounds and pence.

And when you just can't avoid it ...

Of course, with the best will in the world, no parent is ever going to manage to completely avoid going to the supermarket. So if you really have to make a visit, go armed with these tips.

- Go at the quietest times – early morning is good. At least with young children, you are likely to be up, dressed and ready to shop earlier than the rest of the adult population. Or, now that there are more 24-hour supermarkets, if you have a partner who's at home, go at night when the kids are in bed.

- Before you go, snap a picture of your fridge and food cupboards on your phone to remind yourself of what you need to buy.
- Make the deli counter your first port of call – and pick up any free samples of cheese or other snacks to keep children happy as you shop. Some supermarkets now give out free fruit at the entrance to keep kids entertained as they go round.
- Get kids to imagine their own shopping list, and ask them to look for those items as you go round. If they are old enough, let them read the items on your list and help you hunt them down. Children are more likely to eat food when they have had a say in choosing it.
- One of the most stressful moments of a supermarket visit with children has to be the race to unload the trolley and then pack up your items into dozens of bags at the check-out with an impatient queue forming behind you. Now that we are charged for bags, there are even more pressing reasons to find an easier approach. Invest in a set of re-usable shopping bags that you can hang from the sides of the trolleys. They stay open while you shop and when you get to the till, simply lift them out and plonk them onto the conveyor belt. Then re-pack into the same bags on the other side of the cashier. They come in sets of four and are colour-coded too, so you can also sort your groceries as you shop – for example by fruit and veg, frozen and dairy. The other bonus is that you will be able to put everything away more quickly when you get home. They roll up easily, so keep your set in your car.
- Make use of the self-scan-as-you-go handheld machines that some supermarkets offer. Older children can help

beep the items, and then you can place them straight into your bags with no unpacking at the checkout.
- Make shopping fun by going to markets at weekends. Kids are bound to get offered free samples at farmers' markets too. Give them a few pounds to choose what they would like to buy.

And if you really have nothing much left to eat in the house … smile and make a virtue of it. For older children, make a tapas supper by warming up leftovers and serving them up in ramekin dishes or on a platter so that everyone can help themselves.

Getting kids to help out in the kitchen

You might not realise it, but you may already have some willing kitchen helpers. Okay, so they may need a little training; but all too often, we treat our children as helpless little lords and ladies who need to be waited on hand and foot. In fact, we'd be doing them good by allowing them to test their capabilities. Competence breeds confidence and self-reliance, which are qualities many kids never get a chance to develop these days.

At first, it may take a little time, as well as cause a little mess. But you will be training the sous-chefs of the future, and it will improve their motor skills, vocabulary and love of food into the bargain. Here's a rough guide to what children can do at different ages. Remember, if they can use a smartphone, they are capable of switching on the vacuum cleaner or dishwasher.

Age four. Wash fruit and veg. Mash avocado or cooked potato with the back of a fork. Grease pans. Put ingredients into the blender and switch it on to make smoothies or soups.

Age five. Sieve flour and icing sugar. Stir cake ingredients with a wooden spoon. Pour mixtures into moulds. Roll pastry and make shapes. Whisk eggs. Use a pestle and mortar.

Age six. Toast bread. Use a spoon to measure liquids. Stir a mixture in a bowl and spoon it on to baking trays. Cut soft ingredients like butter with a blunt knife.

Age seven. Use scissors to chop herbs. Separate and peel garlic cloves. Peel fruit and veg. Use a serrated knife to chop up soft veg and fruit like strawberries.

Age eight. Grate cheese. Crush garlic with a crusher. Learn to cut an onion with a knife. Stir a mixture in the frying pan under supervision.

Age nine. Use the grill with supervision. Cut up fish with scissors or a knife. Measure out ingredients. Juice fruit. Thread kebabs.

2 Playtime planning:
toys, crafts and TV

Toys, toys, toys. One minute you've started out with a baby rattle and a couple of cuddly animals. The next minute you're knee-deep in the cast of *Frozen* and *Peppa Pig*. Next to cleaning the kitchen and doing the laundry, there is nothing quite like the endless task of picking up playthings to grind an overworked parent down.

There have been times when I literally gasped in horror at the thick lava of puzzle pieces, blocks, bits of dried-out play dough, doll's house furniture and discarded books that spread through my house. But by weeding out the messiest toys, and making sure what's left is organised, you will reduce your workload and have more time to play with your kids instead of picking up after them.

How to head off chaos before it starts

- Many parents are drowning in bits and pieces because their kids simply have too much. The average child gets around 70 new toys a year. So it's inevitable that if you don't have a clear-out, it will quickly become unmanageable. Try the 'one in, one out' rule. Ask your child what toys he doesn't like. Suggest he takes them to a charity shop so that he learns about giving.

- When children are older, motivate them by letting them eBay stuff they no longer want – and then let them use the money to redecorate their rooms.
- Suggest that grandparents and other relatives give their time – or theatre tickets or fun experiences – rather than gifts.
- Think before you buy. Consider how much space a new toy will take up and how long the novelty will last.
- Don't forget: the old-fashioned basics are still the best. A ball, a skipping rope, pencils and some paper will be cheaper, take up less room and encourage your children to be more creative. Don't panic that your kids are losing out on vital educational opportunities because they haven't got the latest all-singing, all-dancing learning game. All Newton needed was a tree and an apple.
- Avoid letting children get into the habit of pulling everything off the shelves – for you to put back. From the age of three, train them to get out a maximum of three games or books at a time. If they want to play with more, they need to return the ones they've used to the proper place.
- Younger children concentrate better when they have just a few good toys instead of too much choice. Keep extra items in boxes marked 'Toys on Holiday', and rotate them. You'll end up doing a lot less tidying.
- Keep messy toys that need adult supervision up and out of the way to avoid disaster. Otherwise, when your back is turned, you risk a felt-tip work of art on your sofa and play dough cement between your floorboards.

- If you have a child who likes jigsaw puzzles, invest in a jigsaw mat so they can roll up and put away half-finished ones instead of leaving them hanging around taking up space. On the same subject, avoid those kids' puzzle books which have a jigsaw per page. They seem like good value at the time, but pieces persistently tumble out and you'll have no choice but to find the right page and painstakingly re-do the jigsaw to put them away.
- Toys can become seriously icky over time. So get fiddly ones (Lego, plastic blocks or small action figures) clean by putting them in a mesh bag and washing them in the dishwasher on a cooler cycle.

Keeping crafts under control

- Don't you just hate those flimsy, floppy plastic containers that so many felt-tips come in? The only way to tidy them away is to slot each one back in, one by one. Cardboard containers will also become dog-eared quickly, forcing you to scrabble around on the floor when all the crayons fall out of the bottom. You'd be better off decanting them into a good-quality shoe box, a Tupperware cutlery divider or even Ziploc bags. Also fantastic are professional make-up artists' boxes with folding drawers; they're like a carry-round craft case.
- Adults, let alone children, have a hard time controlling gloopy glue. It either doesn't come out at all or splurges out all over the table. Where possible use glue-sticks instead. Get a job lot of economy priced ones. It's true that they need their lids, but if they dry up, cut the top off to reveal the fresh stuff underneath.

- The words 'Can I do some painting?' bring many a parent out in a cold sweat. If it's a fine, windless day, let them do it outside where the mess won't matter so much. Get an old wallpaper roll, weigh or tape it down – and let them go for it. If you can't face painting at home at all, take advantage of craft sessions at your local library. They are usually free – and, best of all, the tidying up is someone else's responsibility.

- If you are doing crafts inside, lay out generous amounts of newspaper under all their work so that any mess can be cleared away quickly and scrunched up in the bin, with no sweeping or scooping up.

- Set up a notice board for displaying your child's best drawings, but try to limit the display to ones that show particular flair or are developmental milestones. If your notice board is magnetic, make sure you get the most powerful magnets you can buy, so that the drawings do not drop off. Or hook up a little washing line along one wall and hang up their latest works with clothes pegs. When it's full, edit the pictures down and put the best into a plastic A3 folder or save a picture of them on your phone to make a no-mess digital gallery.

- The same applies to children's 3-D creations, which quickly take up a huge amount of play space. As much as I love my daughters' art, my heart has sometimes sunk at the sight of papier-mâché masks, giant cereal box models, pottery jugs and Easter bonnets they have brought home from school. So after a respectable amount of time, take a picture of your child posing with their work of art as a keepsake – and then ask if it's okay to make room for their new art projects.

Toys to avoid until your child is old enough

Many parents secretly like to think their child is a little bit more advanced for their age. But there are often good developmental reasons why certain toys are only recommended for specific age groups. Not least of which is because they are not grown-up enough to know how to put them away afterwards.

No one wants to stop their child learning new things. But the fact is that if you are too terrified to get out the more challenging games because you can't face the endless fiddly pieces, kids won't play with them anyway, especially if they find them frustrating.

Here are some of the messiest toys – and alternatives that don't take as much tidying up.

Swap: beads for lacing kits. Lacing kits – where your child threads a string through a wooden picture – are just as good as beads for learning hand–eye coordination, and not nearly so fiddly to tidy up afterwards.

Swap: felt-tips for crayons or doodle boards. Until kids are about six, they generally don't put felt-tip lids back on. This leaves you to do it – and you also have the task of weeding out all the dead ones that have dried up. Plus an uncapped felt-tip can cause horrible damage to walls, furniture and upholstery. There are finally new ranges that come – hallelujah – with flip-top lids. Crayons are, anyway, generally easier when children are younger and starting to draw and colour in. But save the packs of a hundred, containing every colour under the sun, until kids really do care about the difference between puce and blush pink.

For younger children, a set of no more than about 12 is quite enough. Limiting the number of colours means that you won't have to chase so many around the house.

With toddlers who are just learning to scribble, you can also save yourself clean-up time by giving them an all-in-one wipe-clean doodle board with a stylus attached. Of course, you will want your child to have something to show for his effort by giving him some paper to draw on too. But a wipe-clean doodle board is perfect for just putting in the practice.

However, don't let them only draw with their fingers on iPads as they will need to develop muscle strength in their hands and motor skills by learning to hold crayons and pencils.

Swap: poster paints for watercolours or use aqua paints. I hate poster paints. They are horrible to pour out, splatter everywhere and then dry up. As soon as your child is old enough, basic watercolours are a much less heavy-handed approach, and they make a tenth of the mess. If your kids really love to splatter, save yourself some clean-up time by buying aquadraw mini-mats. All they need is water to reveal the picture.

Swap: Lego for Duplo or wooden blocks. Children don't really know how to apply the right sort of pressure to build Lego until they are about four – and as the pieces seem to get smaller all the time, they can be hell to clean up afterwards, and even more painful to step on. (Hence the invention of Lego protector slippers.) Until your children are ready, try wooden blocks or Duplo, which are easier to fit together – and also to scoop up.

Swap: flashcards for flip books. If you are intent on teaching your little one their alphabet or want to quiz your primary school-age kids on multiplication, don't buy the loose flashcards, which can easily spill out and spread. Instead opt for the flip-book versions. They are just as good but usually spiral-bound with the question on one side and the answer on the other.

Swap: magnetic toys for Fuzzy-Felt. You might assume a magnet is a magnet. But actually they vary wildly in strength. You may well find that when you buy magnetic books and games, the pictures, letters or numbers are not as magnetic as you might have hoped – and all the pieces are constantly dropping out. Fuzzy-Felt does the same job – and stays put better.

Swap: playworlds for fold-away book versions. Rather than let a plastic or wooden model toy pirate ship or fairyland take over your living room, buy the foldaway 3-D books. They are large fold-out paper versions of farms, palaces, castles and space ships which can just be closed up in an instant with the characters inside, and put away neatly on the bookshelf.

Swap: board games for online versions. On the days when you can't face picking up stray Scrabble letters, chess pieces and Monopoly money – and are also fed up with tip-toeing around unfinished board games – let children play them online, under supervision. Of course, it's better for their motor skills to play the real-life versions, and manipulate the pieces – but for busy days, there are brilliant free versions available on iPads and tablets.

Swap: glitter for glitter glue. We all love glitter, but as a parent, I have discovered that only sand is as good at getting into every nook and cranny and as hard to get rid of. I am embarrassed to say I once found it in my baby's nappy. Let children use the loose stuff at school or at the library – or have a lint roller ready to hoover up fiddly left-over speckles (also, of course, laying out reams of newspaper underneath their craft projects, which you can bin afterwards). At home, stick strictly to glitter glue pens.

Swap: battery-operated toys for wind-up toys. It seems that whenever I have bought something battery-operated for my children, within three months it's lying in a corner gathering dust, waiting for me to organise a battery amnesty. As far as possible, go the old-fashioned route and buy wind-up toys instead. They are usually nicer anyway. Just don't buy the ones with the removable keys or they will inevitably get lost, rendering the toy useless.

How to get toys organised

Now you've pared the toys back to basics, find a place for everything. It will not only speed up your tidying time, it will also enable your kids to help.

- Set up small toy storage areas for younger kids around the house – even if they're just a box that you can wheel behind the sofa or an emptied-out kitchen cabinet – so that they can play close to wherever you are and there is always somewhere to put their games in a hurry.
- Put hooks at your children's level to get stuff out of the way. Have a look at how a nursery school is set up. For example, try hanging coat pegs at kids' height in the hallway to stop them chucking coats on the floor. Hang more hooks in their play areas to hold aprons, best dress-up clothes or anything that could get crumpled and lost if it's stuffed away.

- My test of good storage is whether you can throw in toys (the non-breakable kind, obviously) from about six foot across the room. Make boxes large enough – ideally about a foot deep – but not so huge that they are bottomless pits.
- Also look for containers on wheels that can be rolled out for tidying – and if necessary can be wheeled right to the heart of the worst mess – and then pushed back against the wall or behind the sofa.
- It's a tragic waste not to use the storage space under children's beds, so invest in shallow plastic boxes, again on wheels, which kids can easily roll in and out.
- Label boxes. There's no point having everything beautifully stored if you have to pull it all out to identify what's what. Stick on simple words or, if kids can't read, pictures of what's inside. It means even the littlest children can find what they want, and – crucially – help put it away again.
- Build open, secure low shelves in any alcoves in your child's room. They store much more than ready-made units, children can get what they want and put it back, and there's no risk of them toppling over.
- In the sitting room, consider investing in a toy box that fits into your décor, so it can be quickly reclaimed as an adult space the moment that kids are in bed. Sea-grass or wicker baskets are unobtrusive and light to open – and there's less risk of a heavy lid banging down on little fingers or heads. For safety, get a box with a support to hold the lid open.

How to get kids to help tidy

- Don't be a slave to your children. Experts say that when kids do things for themselves, it builds self-worth. Start early, so that it becomes a fact of life. Remember that by the time children are five, they are able to pick up clothes, put dirty ones in the laundry, straighten duvets, help set and clear the table and put away their toys. Give them these jobs as a special role or grown-up responsibility, instead of making them out to be a boring chore.

- A young child in full flow can create a new mess every minute, so harness that natural energy with some reverse psychology, and make tidying up a game. It may not work perfectly but at least you will feel it's all getting slightly better, not worse. Let them enjoy making a noise as they drop the blocks back into the box. Buy a mini-shopping trolley and suggest they go 'shopping' for toys.
- When you're tidying, give kids a running commentary on what you are doing. As you put things back, explain: 'Your books go in your bookcase.' Putting it into words will reinforce the message. Make the process more imaginative by making the container where they store their princesses into Elsa's Castle or put Star Wars figures into a Death Star.
- With older kids, challenge them to a '10-second tidy' so it doesn't feel like such an onerous task. Crank up the music to get the energy going. If the dust is starting to form a thick coat around their rooms, give kids a pair of old socks and challenge them to see who can collect the most grime.
- Emphasise that your family is a team – and that everyone is responsible for keeping your home a pleasant place to live in. Make them see the advantages by explaining that it helps them to find their things more easily.
- Schedule clean-up time at the same time every day – perhaps the interval just before supper – to get kids into the habit. Choose the 10 minutes before their screen time to get them focused.
- Improve the chances of getting everything in the right place by equipping each bedroom with a generous-sized rubbish and laundry bin. Tell older children that only the clothes that make it to a laundry basket will get washed.

Make it a ritual for them to empty the basket into the main laundry bin at least once a week.

- Keep a drawer as a holding pen for one-off puzzle pieces and bits of Lego until you have time to return them to their proper homes.
- Don't expect perfection. At the end of the day, when you have children you need a family home – not a show house.

Children and screen time

Few parents feel completely okay about putting kids in front of a screen. But it has to be said that when you're really up against it, it's one of the few ways of keeping children busy that doesn't create more mess. Furthermore, with virtually every child in the UK having access to a screen in some form at an earlier age than ever, fretting about technology is about as pointless as worrying about the arrival of the motor car, because it's very much here to stay.

There's also growing evidence that if we are thoughtful, and put well-thought-out limits in place early, rather than using technology as a digital dummy to keep kids quiet, we don't need to feel quite as guilty about it as we were once led to believe. Even the American Academy of Pediatrics has softened its famously hard-line position, previously recommending that there should be no screen time at all before the age of two, and no more than two hours a day for older children.

Professor Jackie Marsh of the University of Sheffield's School of Education has analysed the effects of screens on children from birth to five years old. Following her research, which found that children were using tablets on average one hour and 19 minutes a day, she believes the right age-appropriate apps can help children build a broader range of skills and knowledge. 'When playing some games, they showed problem-solving, prediction, and logic, all skills important for science, technology, engineering and mathematics subjects.'[15] So while children should never spend too much time – no more than an hour a day in total – watching screens, maybe it's time to worry less about the time children spend on such devices, and devote more energy to thinking how that time could be better spent. Just keep a balance and bear in mind that when kids look back on their childhoods, they won't remember their best days of screen time.

Make it interactive. Children will always learn best from human interaction. Don't be fooled into promises that learning apps will make your child smarter or teach them to read. To date, no company has ever been able to produce any evidence showing that is the case. However, when you are tied up, a good two-way story-telling app is fine to keep them busy. The golden rule is not to allow tech to take up the time and brain space children need to learn more vital skills, like open-ended and imaginary play. As brain scientist and molecular biologist John Medina points out: 'The greatest pediatric brain-boosting technology in the world is probably a plain cardboard box, a fresh box of crayons and two hours.'[16]

Draw some boundaries. Make sure that your child realises from early on that there's a time and a place for screens. As discussed elsewhere in the book, there should be no screens at family meals at home, during other times when the family are together – or when the weather presents an opportunity for them to play and run around outside. They should also never have them in their bedroom and they should preferably only be used in common areas of the house.

Put together a watch list. In this day and age, we can pick and choose programming more easily than ever, particularly on YouTube, where you will find kids' shows from every era – as well as an amazing range of educational clips. But of course there's an awful lot there which is not appropriate and can pop up very quickly on the right-hand bar of new videos. With your child, create your own watch list so they have a smorgasbord of viewing you feel is right for them – and say they can only search for and add other content with your permission. You can also subscribe to appropriate channels for them to stick to, and turn on the safety mode by ticking the 'on' button at the bottom of the page. As an extra precaution, set up a family account so you can keep an eye on what they are watching.

Let them earn it. As children get older and need to plan their time more carefully, make it a routine that they only get screen time after homework, but not too close to bedtime. Give them a regular, scheduled slot so they know what they are allowed and it does not become the subject of time-consuming bartering, as it is in many homes. Keep computers in public areas of the house and ask them to put their phones where you can see them so that they don't disappear up to their rooms to text, Snapchat or Instagram.

Virtually guilt-free TV choices for under sevens

Alphablocks

Animated versions of books such as *The Gruffalo* or *Stick Man*

Most David Attenborough wildlife documentaries – but first check that there are no scenes of killing

Horrible Histories

I Can Cook

Messy goes to OKIDO

Mister Maker

My Pet and Me

Nina and the Neurons

Numberjacks

The Numtums

Octonauts

The Snowman or *The Snowman and the Snowdog*

Something Special

Stargazing

Super Why!

Team Umizoomi

3 Morning mayhem:

streamline getting up and out

Mornings can be extremely stressful and manic. With a little thought and planning, you can prevent much of the morning madness.

How to dress your kids in half the time

When buying for children, don't choose clothes just on the basis of how they look. For your own sake, it's essential that their wardrobe is also easy to put on, coordinate and launder. So when they are little, by all means dress your children well – but at the same time, select clothes that make your life a little easier.

- Before you buy, consider how easy a garment will be to put on your child. Clothes with fiddly buttons or zips should be for special occasions only. Elastic waistbands are super-easy – or look for elasticated materials that can be stretched over the head.

- Never buy an outfit that looks remotely creased before you've bought it. If it looks ruffled in the shop, how do you think it will look after a few wears – and when you never get time to iron it?
- The average one-year-old needs up to five outfit changes a day. So look for reversible baby and toddler clothes. Another trick is to dress them in a few light layers. Every time they dirty their top layer, peel it off to reveal a fresh one underneath.
- Buy clothes that do two jobs: coats with hoods for babies so you don't lose hats, and all-in-one body suits so you don't have to worry about socks.
- Check neck openings. Nobody enjoys the struggling and screaming that ensues when you can't get a top over a baby's or toddler's head. So look for boat necks or tops with poppers on the shoulders. Steer very clear of polo and turtle necks.
- Make it fun – sing a song of 'Pop Goes the Weasel' as your child's head comes through – to press home the idea that they'll only be in the dark for an instant. If your child really hates pullovers being yanked down over his head, try cardigans until the phase passes.
- Choose clothes with clues. Look for underwear which has a picture on the front to help kids identify which way round it goes.
- Until children are about five, choose shorter three-quarter sleeve lengths so their cuffs don't get dirty or need to be constantly rolled up when they wash their hands.
- Buy socks in only one colour and style. Harassed parents don't have the time to search for the only other matching colour at the bottom of the sock drawer. If you only buy white from the beginning, most socks will go together, more or less. Buy them in economy packs by the dozen as they vanish into thin air.

- Only buy plain-coloured tights or you will be driven mad when the only pair you can find to go with your daughter's spotty dress are tartan. Play safe with plain colours that go with everything.
- From toddler age upwards, denim is every parent's best friend. It's easy to clean, tough, and goes with anything. The textured colour will hide a host of sins.
- Buy clothes loose and comfy. If your child is between sizes, buy the bigger one. The looser they are, the easier it will be to dress your child – and for your child to dress himself.
- Only let your child choose their outfits within reason. Kids develop their own tastes early. However, it's not a good idea to give in to every little whim, or you will find yourself struggling to talk them out of fancy dress every morning. Instead give them a limited choice by offering two outfits they can choose from, but don't make it a control issue. Unless they are going to be exposed to the elements, it really doesn't matter much at the end of the day.
- Invest in some soft thermal vests. It will save you worrying so much about whether they're keeping their coats buttoned up and scarves on.
- Bear in mind texture when you buy. Anything that's remotely scratchy on the skin will be hated by some small children – and never worn.
- Cut down on those 'challenging' shopping trips. Swap kids' clothes with your friends to save on shopping time and money. Combine a coffee morning or play-date with a swap shop. Keep brochures so you have a quick guide to what's around. Lots of children hate clothes shopping even for themselves – but don't mind earmarking what they want when they see it in a catalogue. Religiously throw out any that are out of date – and keep a tape measure handy so you are not guessing at the sizing.

- Wading through a wardrobe full of clothes that no longer fit your child wastes a lot of time, so take outgrown clothes out of circulation immediately. Keep a box always on hand for items you need to take to the charity shop or which are ready to be passed down to siblings.
- Use the top of wardrobes to store out-of-season clothes that your children don't need to get to – so their current clothes range is pared down and ready to use.

Heading off toilet accidents

- Always run your finger round the leg openings of a baby's nappy to make sure the frill is on the outside – or the poo could leak out. Make sure a boy's penis is pointing down to avoid leaks.
- When you're toilet training, buy pants in bigger sizes, so they are easier for little ones to yank down in a hurry – or leave the bottom half off completely in the early stages when you're at home.
- Don't dress children in dungarees when they are learning to use the loo. They are too fiddly to get on and off. Put boys in trousers with elasticated waists and girls in easy-to-manoeuvre skirts without tights.
- Boys can make an appalling mess while they are trying to perfect their aim. Give them a footstool to give them a fighting chance. Make getting their aim right a game by putting a piece of toilet paper or a little plastic ball in the bowl for target practice. Tell boys they will know they are aiming well if they make a loud weeing noise like daddy.
- Have flushable wipes ready by the toilet for instant wipe-ups and wiping round potties.

- Put a puppy pad under the sheet in case of night-time accidents. If there is an accident you can throw it straight in the bin.
- To avoid your loo looking like the Andrex puppy has been for a visit, draw a line on the wall below which they are not allowed to pull the paper.

Teaching kids to dress themselves

Dressing kids in the morning can be one of the most stressful moments of the day. It can easily descend into tears and tantrums – on both sides – especially if the clock is ticking to get them to the childminder or school.

By the time children are three, they should be starting to help dress themselves in the mornings. Put them on the right road by training them how to do it step by step.

First, ask them to put on their underwear. Help them stick legs into the holes – but let them pull up their pants by themselves. Next, put their top over their head and then let them take over. But don't practise when you are in a rush. Your child is much more likely to become flustered. Instead, have a go when you have a bit more time to spare – maybe at the weekend – and make it fun.

Here are some more tips for helping kids help themselves.

- Tell little ones to sit down when putting on pants, trousers and socks so they don't topple over.
- Encourage youngsters to stick their head in a top first, then put their arms through.

- Spread out tops face-down on the bed so kids will put them on the right way.
- Tell girls to gather up tights around their ankles first, before pulling them up their legs.
- Remind children – and particularly boys doing up trousers – to pull up zips away from their skin so they don't catch.

About shoes

- Don't bother with shoes for babies who aren't walking yet. They look cute, but they're also completely useless and inevitably fall off. Opt instead for good quality baby socks that are also designed to stay on comfortably. In my experience – and that of almost every other parent I know – Gap baby socks usually do the trick. Or try Sock Ons, which are designed to fit over regular socks but keep them in place, no matter how hard your baby kicks and tries to pull them off.
- As children's feet grow, repeat visits to buy new shoes can be time-consuming. Too often you can end up waiting in long queues for someone to measure your child's latest size. And nothing beats the pandemonium of attempting to buy new ones in the run-up to a new school term. Instead buy a shoe measurer or download a child's foot chart off the internet to take the guesswork out of whether kids have outgrown their footwear – and then order shoes online. You can buy plastic versions of the metal shoe measurers they have in shoe shops for as little as £3 on Amazon.
- For girls, patent shoes don't scuff, stay shinier and seem to wear better.
- Save yourself time tracking down shoe polish which exactly matches the colour of your children's shoes, and creates a crumbly mess whenever you use it. Instead polish them with vegetable oil to get rid of scuffs.

- Every parent has wasted vital moments putting shoes on the wrong foot. If this keeps happening, cut a sticker of an animal down the middle – and insert each half in the shoe so they can be matched up correctly.
- Most children do not develop the motor skills to tie their own shoelaces until at least the age of seven. So until then, only buy slip-ons or shoes fastened with Velcro. Your child's carers and teachers will also thank you for it because they don't have time to do up your child's shoe-laces either. If you do lace, double them round the ankle and tie them at the back so there's less chance of the strings being pulled loose. But when they reach the right age, make a concerted effort to teach them this skill.

Keeping laundry to absolute minimum

Keeping kids looking clean and smart can be a real challenge when you are a parent in a rush. All of us want to have some pride in the way our child looks – even though youngsters usually have other ideas. But just a little forethought when you buy your children's clothes will save you an enormous amount of time and fuss down the line.

How to cut down your laundry mountain

- Buy a washer-and-dryer-safe mesh bag for each child's room – one for lights and one for darks. Throw the bags directly into the washing machine and dryer – and the clothes will come out ready-sorted. If your children are old enough, give them back their laundry bag and let them put their garments away themselves.

- If you have younger kids, go one step further when you undress them for the bath, and have a washer-safe bag ready just for socks. Throw the bag in the machine, and then all you'll need to do is pair them up and put them away.
- Have a set of play clothes handy – outfits for kids to wear when they are just at home getting mucky or playing – like some sweat pants and a loose sweatshirt that don't need washing every time they're worn. The children will be able to relax and so will you.
- Buy plain fabric T-shirts where possible. Any transfer characters on the front may well come off after a few washes. Otherwise turn them inside out before you put them in the wash.
- From around the age of two, train your children not to wipe their nose or mouth on their sleeve. Instead get them into good habits by giving them a piece of paper towel at every meal so they don't wipe mucky hands and faces on clothes.
- Do more spot-cleaning. Just because your child's school sweatshirt has been worn once, it doesn't necessarily need washing right away. As long as it's stain-free and the cuffs and necklines aren't too grimy, it can be worn a second time.
- Train children not to throw their clothes on the floor. Apart from making a mess, it makes you feel that you've automatically got to wash them. At first, little ones will enjoy the grown-up responsibility. Of course it will wear off with older kids, so warn them that anything dumped on the ground will be confiscated.
- More and more primary schools are asking kids to wear a uniform. While it's essential to pare a wardrobe down to the basics, this is one area where you need plenty of spares so you're not constantly laundering the only two you

own – or hunting for them when they go missing. Accept hand-me-downs with open arms and go to second-hand uniform sales so you always have extras.

Name tags

When kids get to school age, attaching name tags becomes a never-ending job. But they are worth the effort for the amount of time they save tracking down lost clothes. Here are some of the speediest choices.

- Forget sewing. Buy an indelible laundry pen so that you can mark your child's property instantly. Put your phone number on the insides of coats and hats so anyone who finds them can contact you. Sharpie pens are brilliant for this as you can use them to write on any item from school bags to folders – and they don't bleed. If you are in a rush, only write your surname – unless it's incredibly common.

- Some parents have told me that they find it calming and nostalgic to stitch round name tags. Fine, but if that's not you and you've only got one minute, instead loop the name tag round and put several secure stitches at one end.

- Even quicker, buy clip-on tags, now available on the internet. Simply cut the label, fold it and fix it in place with its special rivet. The tags won't irritate the skin and can be washed at high temperatures.

- Keep iron-on tags next to your ironing pile – and affix them as you work through it – though be warned that they do have a reputation for falling off after repeated washes. Keep them for items that don't need laundering so much, like coats, scarves and bags.

How to get through your laundry faster

Every parent knows the panic when they realise the one item of clothing their child needs that morning is buried so deep at the bottom of the laundry pile it would take an industrial digger to get it out. Or the depressing sight of an insurmountable ironing pile in the corner. But there are ways of keeping washing and ironing to a minimum.

- Never buy kids' clothing based solely on whether your child will look cute in it. First have a good think about how easily the clothes will be to look after. Try crunching a section of the material and seeing what happens. If it creases easily, put it back – simple as that. Avoid fabrics like linen. Instead go for stretchy materials like velveteen, thicker cottons and elastane/rayon mixes which will be wearable straight out of the washing machine.
- When choosing a new machine, look for a model with an optional quick wash cycle setting for emergencies. Otherwise you could be waiting up to two hours to get one cycle done.
- Train older kids in the habit of checking there are no tissues left in their pockets before they put them in the laundry basket – or you'll be picking scraps off the whole washing load.
- Keep everything you need near the washing machine, on a shelf preferably at eye level. Arrange products from left to right in the order you use them. For example, start with stain removers, then follow with bleaches and detergent, then fabric softener.
- In terms of making mess, washing powder is the worst, especially as it seems to get everywhere and gunks up your dispenser drawer. Instead use powder tablets or, best of all, gel tablets that go straight in the drum. Also worth

a try are washing machine balls which promise to clean clothes without detergent by increasing the pH of the water. They should be mess-free.

- Easy-iron fabric conditioners will also make clothes softer, more manageable and easier to press.

How to dry clothes so you don't have to iron

- If you can, take clothes out of the machine as soon as the washing or tumble drying cycle has finished. If they are set solid, put them back in the washing machine on a short cycle with a wet item to make them flexible again.
- Hang clothes like shirts immediately for the wrinkles to drop out. Fold the rest flat and smooth as soon as the cycle ends, while the clothes are still warm. The warmth will help you to smooth out the wrinkles.
- Get the biggest drying rack you have room for. Nothing is more annoying and time-consuming than trying to make space around your home for wet laundry. If you have room, hang a laundry rack from the ceiling near your washing machine or, at the very least, put up some hooks so you can hang clothes straight out of the machine. Strangely, although many of us have a setting on our machines called Easy Iron, few of us use it. It works by injecting a flow of cooler air through the clothes towards the end of the cycle, and cutting the likelihood of wrinkles.
- Don't jam the clothes into your washing machine. The more clothes are squashed, the more creased they will come out. Keep heavy items like towels separate – or they will press on the lighter ones and wrinkle them.

- If you hang clothes on the washing line properly, you can really cut down on your ironing duties. Hang clothes with the heavier part of the garment downwards. That way gravity will pull many of the wrinkles out.
- If you have the room, hang laundry as stretched out horizontally as possible and try not to fold it over the washing line. Use three pegs for the sides and middle and hang up each item separately without overlapping it with the next.

How to rush through the ironing you have left

In a recent survey of parents, ironing came second in the list of most hated tasks – with 62% saying that it was the worst chore after picking up toys.[17] Here are a few ways to reduce the pain.

- Avoid buying clothes – for you and the children – that have too many buttons. They'll just slow your ironing down.
- Before you start, divide your ironing piles according to their ironing temperatures. Start with the coolest temperature clothes first while the iron's heating up. If you are in a hurry, don't turn up the temperature – you will regret it when the surface meets the wrong sort of fabric.
- Put a layer of tin foil underneath your ironing board cover. It will reflect heat and speed up the process.
- Get the right iron. Is it reasonably light and easy to move around? Has it got a good tip so it can reach into those corners?
- Use the steam option. Make sure it provides a steady supply of steam as this can really save time. Otherwise buy a hand-held steamer (these can cost as little as £25),

which will save you getting out the ironing board in emergencies.

- Get the board at the right height. You need to apply the right pressure when you are ironing, so don't have it too high. If it is too low, your back will ache.
- Don't iron things that don't need to be ironed. That includes socks, underwear and towels. Instead of doing the sheets, only do the pillow cases, which are more visible.
- Think about buying ironing water. It will stop your iron fuzzing up, and makes your clothes smell lovely. It also contains moisturisers to make textiles easier to press.
- Iron shirt seams on the wrong side first. If you are pushed for time, only do the collars.

The school run

Without a doubt, when children get to school age, many parents' most hectic part of the day is the school run. This is a challenge which truly defines the word multi-tasking. As well as getting yourself washed, dressed and looking presentable, the children also have to be fed, watered, groomed and teamed up with homework and sports kits.

But there are ways to get manic mornings under control.

- Lay out everyone's clothes – including your own – the night before so you aren't rooting around for your only decent pair of tights while chaos is unfolding all around you. If you can, get yourself dressed before getting the kids up – if you're telling them off for being in their pyjamas when you're still wrapped in a towel, the situation will rapidly deteriorate. Once dressed, slip on your dressing gown over your clothes, so you don't get covered in breakfast spills.

- Coax reluctant children out of bed on cold mornings by laying out their school clothes on the radiator to warm them up. Or use music. One mum I know has a system which pipes music to every room in the house – and wakes her three children up simultaneously with a blast of ABBA.
- If children are tired and won't get out of bed, move their bedtime back by an hour. Experts recommend that kids aged up to 12 should get between 10 and 12 hours' sleep, but studies are showing that British children are becoming chronically sleep-deprived. In particular, check that older kids aren't burning the midnight oil on their phones and tablets. If they are over-tired, they will be grumpy the next morning, making the morning run much harder.
- One of the most effective ways to wake children is to open the curtains. Natural light has been found to stimulate the brain to release the hormones that naturally wake them up. Failing that, and in winter, turn the light on.
- Agreeing at bedtime what kids are wearing the next day is especially important if they don't wear a uniform. Get them involved by asking them to Google the weather forecast the night before. Tell them any decision made the previous evening is final.
- When the weather is mild, short socks are much quicker to put on than knee-length ones.
- Make hurrying up a game for the younger ones. To speed your child along when necessary, set a timer and say: 'Let's try and get dressed before the buzzer goes off.'
- If your kids are old enough to tell the time, trying turning the clocks forward 10 minutes. The children will get a move on, but you won't be rushing around like a mad person.
- Get your children to do the same things in the same order every morning – getting dressed, brushing hair and teeth,

and so on. They will soon learn automatically what they need to do next – and save you the nagging.

- Make sure toothbrushes and toothpaste are in reach for younger kids. Help little ones to stand at the sink and wash themselves by buying an anti-slip bathroom stool. Check taps are set so the water never gets too hot to hurt them.
- Draw up a list of what they need to take to school on each day. Write it on your kitchen blackboard so that they can consider what they need to collect up while they eat their breakfast.
- Invest in a full-length mirror. Instead of fidgeting when you try to dress and brush their hair, you will find your children are more likely to stand still and watch their reflection while you try to groom them.
- If they are over the age of six, put out breakfast things like cereal (with the spoons in a jar in the middle of the table) so that kids can help themselves. If you're not ready to make it to the kitchen, they can get a head start.
- Have easy over-the-head aprons handy for those school mornings when you are serving porridge or other messy foods which might stain their outfits. If you are doing eggs, try them hard boiled so there is less risk of getting runny egg yolk on school clothes.
- At a time when they are not begging, talk through with younger kids why it's never a good idea to take favourite toys to school. You will find they focus on the toy, rather than leaving the house. When it gets forgotten at the end of the day – or, worse still, lost or taken home by another child – you will have a drama on your hands.
- Have everything you need – book bags, gym kit, library books – at hand by the door. It's so easy to forget things when you're in a hurry.

- Put up a hook somewhere convenient and get in the habit of automatically putting your keys there to avoid panicky searches for the car keys when it's time to leave. That way they won't get left on sideboards and covered over with mail, papers or other debris.
- Cut down the time you spend zipping and buttoning kids' coats by buying ponchos, preferably with a hood, which they can throw on over anything in an instant.
- Teach kids how to pull down their cuffs when they are putting on coats so their sleeves don't get uncomfortably scrunched up in those vital last moments before leaving the house.
- Threading gloves on strings through kids' coats usually just leads to tangles. Get some mitt clips – strips of elastic with clips at each end – to keep gloves attached to sleeves and ready to put on. Old suspender clips will also work.
- Thread scarves through coat loops, so they are ready to wrap round your child's neck as soon as he puts it on.
- If you drive to school, stock up your car's glove compartment with cereal bars, oat cakes or dried fruit for late mornings, so at least you can top up on breakfast if you've fallen behind. Also keep a supply of wipes handy to clean up any messy faces or food stains left over from breakfast. If you walk to school, keep the supplies in the bottom of a younger child's pram or in your bag.
- If you are running behind, speed up the walk to school by letting your older child take their scooter, as long as there is somewhere to park it at school. (Make it distinctive by putting on stickers or ribbons – so many scooters look alike and they often get taken home by the wrong child by mistake.) Instead of your child dragging along behind you, you will be struggling to keep up.

How to fix your child's hair faster

If you have daughters, you will know how much screaming and shouting can accompany even the most harmless attempts to get your girls groomed. Try these shortcuts to get through it with less trauma.

- When they are little and their hair is baby fine, get the softest bristle brush you can find so your daughters aren't afraid of getting scratched on the face with bristles. When they are older, use wide paddle brushes to get the job done more efficiently.

- Avoid novelty accessories. Anything with too much ornamentation can easily get tangled up in girls' hair. Don't use any accessories that are too heavy either. They will slip and dangle, and pull out delicate hair with them.

- Avoid bands with metal bits – they break the hair. Instead buy thick comfy towelling ones that won't get so easily tangled.

- Parents of daughters with long hair will know the everlasting hunt for hair bands. Have a range constantly to hand by wrapping them around the end of hairbrushes.

- To make it easier the next morning, put their hair in loose braids at bedtime to keep it neat and knot-free for the following morning.

- If you find a bad knot, pull it apart with your fingers first. Then spray it with spray-on conditioner. To avoid making it worse and forcing the hair into a tighter bundle, start from the bottom of the tangle with a wide-tooth comb and work your way up. Hold your child's hair away from the roots to stop it tugging and hurting.

- The starting point for a child's hairstyle is the parting. First sweep the hair from side to side to see where the parting falls naturally. Then develop the rough line with the thin end of a comb. Don't make the mistake of assuming that all partings lie in the middle. You will just be fighting a losing battle.

- Keep a pair of hair cutting scissors at home to trim long hair every few weeks. That way you may only need to go to the hairdresser every three months for a 'shape'. Play hair salons to make it more fun, but make it clear it's a game they should only play with grown-ups. I say this after my four-year-old walked into the room once with her shoulder-length mane hacked into a pudding bowl.

- Tell kids you are taking them for a 'trim' not 'a cut' or some will get frightened of what it will entail.

- When hair brushes, combs and accessories get dirty, remove the hair, throw into a mesh bag and place in the washing-machine.

The frantic world of extracurricular activities

As the pressure mounts to get our children to achieve more earlier, it's tempting to put them into every extracurricular class going. But that's not only expensive, it's also stressful for you to get them to the classes on time and pay for them.

In the current hothouse educational atmosphere, parents often tend to sign children up far too early and for far too many classes. As with the educational toy companies, businesses have been very quick to cash in on parents' fears that they can never do enough for their children, convincing them that some of the things that kids would do naturally – if they were given the time and space – should be taught by 'professionals'.

There are, of course, benefits. Getting children successfully involved in the right sort of sport for them, for example, has been associated with higher levels of self-confidence and academic performance, more involvement with school, fewer behaviour problems and lower likelihood of drug-taking and risky sexual behaviour.

But if after-school activities are allowed to become scattergun, there is a price to pay. Our stress levels rise as we become social secretaries, juggling complex schedules worthy of a CEO and paying ever-higher fees – and all this before they've even started their homework.

A recent study found that over-anxious parents are making children 'work' for more than 54 hours a week[18] – more than the average adult spends in the office – even though it's essential that children also have down time to process what they are learning.

Here's how to step off the bandwagon.

Don't start too young. Young children need their parents most of all, and will learn more from fun interaction with you than from an organised music class or baby gym sessions. Doing too much, surrounded by too many children, can make babies and toddlers clingy and insecure. For them, a trip to the park is just as exciting. Also ask yourself if you are creating a busy timetable because you are not sure what to do with them at home. Make sure that any groups you do join are not too large and are manageable for young children.

Keep it in school. Steer children towards extracurricular activities they can do at school, preferably at break or lunch times. That way there is no commuting involved, there is more free time and children can get a taste for what they might be good at with less financial pressure on you.

Don't fret over giving up. Even if children give up instruments or other skills after years of lessons and practice, they have not wasted their time because they will still have learnt a great deal. Remember, too, that children learn from quitting. They learn to admit when they have too much on their plates.

Hold your nerve. Leaving our children to their own devices in this day and age has come to be seen as neglectful. But some children are just happier playing at home. Never assume you are doing nothing by not signing your kids up to the latest trendy class. See it as making a conscious decision to let them find out more about themselves through play, which is the natural way children learn.

4 Behaving better:

easier ways to encourage good behaviour

When you've got loads on your plate, you want the time with your kids to be rewarding and enjoyable, not a marathon of nagging, whingeing and bartering. Dare you imagine how much valuable time you would save if your children did what you asked – when you asked them to do it?

Of course, like everything in parenting, it's easier in principle than in practice. But it will definitely spare you and your children endless rows and tantrums if you sit down and consciously decide what your expectations are – and lay them out for everyone to agree, respect and remember.

If you stick to the basics – and make sure the kids know how they are expected to behave – you might even get them to listen the first time instead of the fifteenth.

A less stressful approach to teaching children good behaviour

Many parents make discipline more time-consuming and stressful than it really needs to be. They expend a lot of energy endlessly barking orders at children and telling them what *not* to do instead of noticing and acknowledging them for doing something right. Children want to please – so you will find that training them with positive attention instead of negative will be less stressful for both you and your kids. The more you tell them what they are doing correctly, the easier they will become.

Furthermore, my view is that star charts are overly complicated, time-consuming and often hard to stick to. They tend to be too scattergun, trying to fix all sorts of different types of behaviour, which can be confusing and demotivating for a young child. To keep it clear in your mind – and in theirs – concentrate on just one type of behaviour you'd like to change, like going to bed on time.

If you are going to reward them, make it a simple system or it will get too complicated to remember what you owe them. Instead make it immediate and visual. For example, putting a stone in a glass jar in the kitchen each time they do what they are meant to – until they get enough for a treat – is a simple way for both you and them to keep on track.

But perhaps the most sure-fire way to ensure good behaviour is to set aside chunks of dedicated special time at around the same time every day so they are not acting up to win your attention. It need not be more than 10 minutes in one go. But let them be in charge and allow them to direct the play – and tell them this time is only for them. This satisfies their need for control so they'll be less likely to try to seize it at other times.

The seven most common sins of harassed parents

1. Shouting to get kids to do things

Time-wasting. Yelling at the top of your voice may work the first time – by stunning children into submission. It's a default that many of us resort to, especially when we are tired and stressed – and we fool ourselves that a 'shock and awe' moment will jolt them into doing the thing we want them to do or 'really teach them a lesson'.

The truth is that the novelty quickly wears off and you'll simply teach them to switch off and close down – or scream back at you. Plus you'll waste your own time and destroy your peace of mind by feeling like a terrible parent afterwards.

If it keeps happening, work out what fuels your outbursts. Learn to spot the signs that you are about to lose it and the reptilian, reactive part of your brain is about to take over.

Unless it's a total emergency and your child is harming or seriously upsetting a sibling, leave the room for a minute or so and take some deep breaths – there is nothing to be gained from exploding. Remember you always have a choice – and you always need to stay the adult. See yelling as a useful barometer of how you are feeling. If you start noticing yourself shouting more, it's probably a sign that you need to take some deliberate steps to look after yourself and de-stress.

Even if you are not telling them off, shouting at kids from another room to chivvy them into brushing their teeth or getting dressed is also a waste of time. You are simply giving them the chance to say they can't hear you. Pretty quickly, it escalates into an exasperated shouting fest.

Time-saving. As far as is realistically possible, stop what you are doing for a moment, go into the room where they are, make eye contact and tell them what you want in a low, clear, authoritative voice, which gives the message that you expect them to do it, not that you don't. If necessary, get down on their level, so they know you mean business. A little eye contact goes a long way.

2. Not being clear about the rules

Time-wasting. If you make up rules on an ad hoc as-and-when basis, you will confuse your kids. You will also be inviting time-consuming conflict, because your children will think they have got room for manoeuvre and will try to argue the point. If you are feeling a bit tired and fuzzy, you may also forget exactly what you said before – leaving your kids to push the boundaries even further to see where they lie.

Time-saving. Head off conflict by setting out your house rules in advance and sticking to them. Let older children have some input so it all feels more democratic – and tell them that the adults will be abiding by them too. Make the rules realistic for the ages of your children. Then write the list on a large, colourful piece of paper and stick it where the whole family can see it.

Writing the rules down in black and white also means you and your partner will be on the same page, as will any caregivers who come into your home, like grandparents and babysitters. You will also probably want to refer to the list when your own resolve is feeling a bit shaky and you've had a long day. The rules become the bottom line which your children know they can't argue with.

Ask the children to suggest some of the rules and work out themselves – with your help – why yours are important. If kids are old enough, hold a family meeting to discuss them. Make them positive, not negative, instructions so they feel more positive. Underline the fact that they apply to everyone in the home – even the grown-ups – so they feel fair. Give plenty of acknowledgement and praise when children stick to them.

Each home is different, and the rules may need to be re-drawn slightly as new challenges arrive. But this a starter list for a family with children, from toddler age to about eight.

1. We are gentle. We do not hurt, push or hit each other.
2. We are kind. We treat others as we would like to be treated.
3. We do our homework without making excuses.
4. We use our pleasant voices to be heard.
5. We understand that sometimes we have to wait patiently.
6. We help put our toys away and keep our rooms tidy.

7. We tell the truth and talk to our parents if something is bothering us.
8. We remember that our family is a team so we can help each other to have a home that we can all enjoy.

3. Negotiating too much

Time-wasting. Although many parents believe they are being sensitive and inclusive by letting children have an opinion on everything from what to eat to what to wear, it can be frightening for a youngster to have too much power. No child wants to be more in charge than a grown-up.

Time-saving. You can, however, give them a restricted selection of choices. For example: 'You can stay inside and do some drawing or go outside and play football. Which of these two things do you want to do?' Let them choose between two equally good options. They don't have to know that you'd be happy with whichever one they opt for.

4. Entering into a debate

Time-wasting. The other mistake parents make is allowing requests to sound optional. If you want your child to have a bath, but it comes out sounding like a question, your child may take advantage by saying no – and you will have a row on your hands.

Time-saving. Once you have made your decision, keep any explanation brief. If absolutely necessary, make direct eye contact and state clearly in fewer than 20 words why that's the rule. At neutral times, when there's no row going on, talk through with your child the reason that rule is in place. Prepare for any typical flashpoints – like tidying up or bedtime – before they blow up, by discussing how you would like it to go. When the child can imagine and rehearse in their minds how you want them to behave, and can foresee how pleased you will be when they do, they are more likely to do it your way.

5. Giving in

Time-wasting. If you work, time pressures can mean that in the limited hours you have with your kids, you want to make it all 'perfect' and conflict-free. Parents can also fall into the trap of thinking that saying yes to their children all the time makes their kids happy. The problem becomes worse, say experts, when parents who were brought up in a very disciplinarian way decide to behave the opposite way with their own kids.

Time-saving. Set limits and stick to them. Otherwise children will feel unsafe and will push you to see what you are going to do about it. Remember that, as a parent, if you never say no, you are not doing your job properly.

6. Feeling guilty

Time-wasting. So many parents start off well in laying down the law – and then ruin it by worrying that they have been unfair when the child cries and screams. Because as adults we know we would have to be seriously upset to become so hysterical, we fear we must have gone over the top when kids shed tears. The fact is that younger children can weep at the drop of a hat. That's the way they are wired. Many's the time when I have been amazed by seeing my kids developing a tantrum from zero to 60 – and just as rapidly going back to zero again.

Time-saving. Stick to your guns. Unless you are stressed or have completely got the wrong end of the stick, your initial instincts were probably right. Pretend you are somewhere else if you have to, or go into autopilot to hold your line. Even walk away, because nothing will be gained if you explode. Make it clear that when mummy or daddy says no, they really mean no. If necessary, repeat it like a mantra until they get the message. Otherwise clear your diary for an endless round of exhausting tantrums and whinge-fests – and I mean exhausting for you, not them.

7. Feeding children snack foods

Time-wasting. When we hear the words 'I'm hungry' many of us feel duty bound to swing into action. For the sake of a quiet life, you may have also fallen into the trap of feeding them a constant stream of snack foods like crisps or biscuits. But although they may be happy for a moment, it's not long before the sugar content sends their insulin levels on a roller coaster, creating hyperactivity – followed by more hunger pangs. Before you know it, they are back again wanting more.

Time-saving. Give kids slow-release protein snacks like apple slices topped with peanut butter or a turkey–cheese roll-up, which can be just as tasty as instant snacks. Their blood sugar levels will even out, they will calm down and they'll be fuller for longer.

How to stop kids whining

Whining not only shatters the nerves of every hassled parent. It also eats up an amazing amount of time.

Make no mistake. The drip, drip, drip is meant to grind you down until you can't take it a second longer. But bear in mind that they wouldn't do it unless it had worked in the past. So if you want an end to this time drain, here's how to head it off before it starts.

- Ask children not to use 'the whiny voice', and tell them it's because you can't understand them. Draw attention to how it sounds by talking back to them in the same tone. Instruct them to use their normal voice instead and thank them for asking nicely.
- Nip whingeing in the bud by acknowledging what kids are asking for the first time they say it. In the same way as you expect them to listen to you the first time, make sure you listen to them too. Show them you have heard them by looking at them, repeating what they have just said and giving the appropriate response. Even if it's not the answer they want, they will ease off once they know the message has got through.
- Always deliver on promises. If you say you are coming to play with them, honour it. Don't kid yourself you can squeeze in five minutes of housework first without them noticing, however worthy your aim. Otherwise they won't trust you to do what you say – and will become even whinier.
- Check what TV they are watching. You might be surprised by some of the undesirable behaviour of some of the characters. Programme makers may well argue that there's a moral at the end of the show, but your child is more likely to take away the bratty behaviour than the life lesson.
- Watch your own whining. Are you constantly moaning to your partner, tutting, sighing, huffing and raising your

eyes to the heavens? Be honest and double check that your children are not learning bad habits from you. Try to go a day without complaining to start with – and then keep going.

- If older children have a more general complaint – for example, that they are not allowed the same privileges as their friends – ask them to write it all down so that you can really hear what they are saying without it descending into a row. It will get it out of their system – and once it's down in black and white, it may not seem so serious to them after all. They will also feel that you are taking their grievances seriously.
- Use humour to break the mood. Tell *them* how you want a million pounds, a new car, a designer wardrobe and all the rest. Children need to learn they won't get everything they want in life. If they say life's not fair, agree. It's also not fair that there are children in the world with hardly anything to eat and nowhere to live.
- Teach them gratitude. Two generations ago, a child might have owned one or two treasured soft playthings. Now they are likely to have a range of hundreds of different branded items and toys. A Unicef report found that British parents were trapping their children in a cycle of 'compulsive consumerism' by showering them with things, rather than spending time with them.[19] However, our children are not getting happier as a result, and they are actually likely to have higher levels of satisfaction with life if we train them to appreciate what they already have by modelling grateful behaviour ourselves. In one experiment on 11- to 13-year-olds, two groups of pupils kept a diary for two weeks. One set was asked to write five things they were grateful for. The other was asked to write five things that annoyed them. Three weeks afterwards, the students

who counted their blessings were still reporting feeling happier with their lives than their peers.[20] It need not take time if you weave recognising the good things in their lives into your everyday conversations with them. As soon as they are old enough to look back over their day, ask them for one nice thing that happened to them. It will help the whole family gain a more positive outlook.

Other time-consuming hassles you don't need

Lending and borrowing toys. 'Neither a borrower nor a lender be' doesn't just apply to money. It applies to toys too. By all means get kids into good habits by letting them share on play-dates, but discourage them from taking other children's toys from the house. If another child offers to let them take one home, just decline politely – and say your child will look forward to coming to play with the item next time. Having the responsibility of looking after another child's property will eventually boil down to you – and returning it in one piece is one more thing you don't need on your overloaded to-do list. With older children, a lending and borrowing ban also saves all sorts of misunderstandings.

Swapping toys. This can also apply to siblings too. In my house, there used to be endless bartering and promises about what the other child can keep for ever and ever, followed by rows over who really owns what. Sharing is fine – but when toys get given away, everyone loses track, and the flare-ups begin again.

Making yourself a doormat. To begin with, whenever my three-year-old dropped something, she would demand I pick it up – although she was quite capable of doing it herself. It quickly became clear she regarded treating mummy like a slave as entertaining – until I made it a general house rule that whoever drops an object retrieves it. Remember that kids would have you waiting on them hand and foot forever if they could get away with it, and children don't respect servants – they just give them more work to do. So don't make more work for yourself by being a walk-over.

How to stop sibling rivalry

Sibling rivalry is not all bad – it teaches children how to negotiate, share and stand up for themselves. But there are times when you, as a hassled parent, find listening to kids bickering over toys, calling each other names or hitting each other beyond exhausting.

If your head's already overloaded, the added stress of hearing 'Mummy, he hit me' for the tenth time can frankly be the final straw. Of course, there is a whole library of books on the subject – but as you don't have the time to read them, this is basically what you need to know.

Talk to them. A large part of sibling rows is indignation. So take each child aside at a quiet time and ask them for their point of view. Make them see that you understand how they feel when their brothers and sisters annoy them. Tell them what it was like for you growing up with your siblings if it helps. At the same time, also explain how the other child feels when they ignore, shout at or snatch from them.

Ask them to sort it out. With older children, you can ask them to negotiate the solution themselves. Listen to both sides equally, acknowledge what each has to say, and tell them you have confidence that they will work it out. Come back later and find how they did – and if it was successful, explain exactly what they did right.

Don't dodge the issue. Stop repeating the mantra 'You have to love your brother(s) and/or sister(s)' because this only causes more resentment and will add to their frustration. At a quiet time, ask them precisely why they are unhappy with their siblings. It might yield an explanation you'd never dreamed of. For a time, my six-year-old daughter Lily was behaving aggressively towards her little sister. When asked why, she explained that she didn't like the fact that Clio could be at home with me after morning nursery was finished, while Lily had to stay at school until 4pm. So it was really a plea for more time with us. When we fitted it in, her resentment of her sister dissipated. Ask questions to get to what is really going on and help them give their feelings a name so that they can make sense of them and feel more in control of their emotions.

Set boundaries. Sit down with your children and discuss how they would like to be treated by a sibling – and how they should behave back. But make sure they know the bottom line – that it's never acceptable to snatch, bite or push. Tell them that it's fine to vent anger, but not through violence – and help find them another outlet, like kicking a football or pummelling a cushion.

Notice what they are doing well. When siblings are sharing or just enjoying an activity together, make a point of acknowledging it. Say things like, 'I see the way you have helped each other to make a new house for your action figures.' It will make them more likely to repeat the behaviour.

Give them time on their own. Ask yourself honestly if you are really giving each child enough attention on their own. Ask them to come with you on an errand to the shops, for a walk in the park together or to play a board game – but make a point of telling them it's because you want to spend some time only with them. It can be miraculous how quickly this transforms a sulky, bolshy youngster into an angel because he doesn't have to share you – and has you to himself.

Never compare. Make each child feel special in a different way and help them develop different talents. Sensitive kids are often looking to keep score and spot slights against them, so make sure you show the same positive body language and facial expressions to each child.

Encourage teamwork. Let them play on a team against you and your partner, or encourage them to form a band. Show them how they can help each other. When one child hurts himself, ask his sibling to look after him. Ask the older child to help the younger one with something they can't do. When I asked my eldest daughter to design my younger child's nativity play costume, they spent hours happily trying out different angel outfits – and Lily's general irritation with her sister was turned into pride. Foster some team spirit – and make it clear that everyone in your household is on the same side.

How to get kids to do homework without a row

For many parents, after the school run, dealing with homework is the most stressful part of the day – a nightly battle they could really do without.

Evenings should ideally be precious times when parents can reconnect with kids – not a time-consuming battle of wills, especially when you have had a long day as well.

But getting children to do their homework has never been harder with the lure of smartphones, video games and social networks. So unless you work out a plan, you have a recipe for nerve-jangling nightly melt-downs. Set out to reduce the flashpoints from the start.

First find out how long they are supposed to be spending on the homework, according to the teacher, says Noël Janis-Norton, author of the essential handbook *Calmer, Easier, Happier Homework* (Hodder, 2013): 'That makes it clear from the start how much time is available. Within a day or two, they will start completing it in the period allowed because it feels like a job they have to get done.'

Find the time of the day after school that works best for your child – either straight after arriving home or after a short break. Agree a start time every day so that the rule turns into a routine and there is less room for resistance and negotiation.

To make sure it's done as well as it can be, but without doing it for them, Noël also suggests a talk-through: five minutes when you ask your child questions about what they need to do to do a good job.

Because their lesson will seem a long time ago, refresh your child's memory by asking them questions like 'Do you need to write full sentences?' or 'Do you have to show your working?'

'I need help!' is of course the cry that every parent dreads. When they hear this, many stressed-out parents will end up doing the homework because they are just so desperate to get it over with. But remember that homework is your child's job, not yours. Doing it for them just masks any problems your child might be having and gets you dragged into a nightly conflict.

Of course, there is still the possibility that the work really is too hard for them, or that they have missed a step and don't understand. If so, check with their teacher. 'Remember, the job of the teachers is to teach,' says Noël. 'The job of the parent is to teach good habits. Children are only learning when it's their brain that's coming up with the answers.' Here are some other ways to get homework done with less fuss.

Start homework at roughly the same time every day. The key reason youngsters work at school without complaining is that their day is organised for them. They know when and where they will be doing their lessons and how long they have to complete tasks. To get them to do homework with no rows, the same should apply when they get home – so set aside 'sacred time'.

Set up a homework centre. For older children, make a special place for study that includes a desk, sharpened pencils, rubbers and reference books. Don't assume the best place is the bedroom because it can be hard to concentrate in the room where you play and sleep. Computer homework should also be done in communal areas so you know they are not using it for anything else.

Keep them equipped. Buy them pencils with rubbers at the end, so they are not searching for an eraser to correct mistakes. Don't skimp on cheap pencil sharpeners either;

the budget plastic ones just splinter pencils. Instead invest in a substantial heavy-duty model, with a collecting barrel attached, so the shavings don't fall on the floor.

Keep it positive. Praise your youngster when they're trying hard, especially when they find it difficult. If they get it correct, say, 'You got there.' If they make a mistake, say 'Nearly,' and let them have another go. Praise their effort and perseverance. Step away if you feel yourself becoming exasperated. Otherwise they will feel criticised and they will start avoiding homework for fear of disappointing you.

Talk to the teacher. If your child has weekly tests to revise for, ask the teacher what learning style suits them best. Children learn in different ways. Some learn by seeing and reading, others by hearing or writing words down. So there may be lots of other ways to learn, such as making words out of play dough or turning the times tables into a song, which will be more fun for everyone.

How to get kids to do what they need to – without being asked a hundred times

Teeth brushing

- As soon as your child picks up their toothbrush, notice and acknowledge that they've started the process. It works much better to praise children for what they are doing than tell them off for what they aren't.
- Make it more fun by letting your younger kids choose their own special toothbrushes – and even their own brand of kids' toothpaste – to make them feel proud and involved.

- Make up a tooth-brushing song – or really go the whole hog and buy an electric toothbrush that plays a tune to keep him scrubbing. Or buy a toothbrush holder egg timer to keep them brushing for three minutes.
- Little ones don't really see the point of brushing teeth. So show them one of the animated videos online explaining there are invisible bugs on the surface they need to battle to keep them from making holes. Explain too that they will be scrubbing off the yellow – and getting minty fresh breath and pearly white teeth instead.
- Be a good role model. Clean your teeth at the same time and ask your child to play copy-cat with you.

Hairwashing and bathtime

Almost every child goes through a phase when they scream blue murder each time you come near them to wash their hair. I have literally seen my kids turn into the demon from *The Exorcist* – biting and clawing to get out of the bath when I have come near them with a glob of shampoo, as if I was trying to murder them, not keep them clean. Still, it has to be done. So for your own sake, as well as theirs, make it as painless and fuss-free as possible. Here are some strategies to try.

Cut down on hair washes. Until they start producing more oil from their scalps, young children can go at least a week without one.

Don't use force. When you are tired and stressed and your child is kicking up hell, it's tempting to restrain them while you get the job done to get it over with as quickly as possible – but this just compounds the problem. If you feel this is a risk, try to pick a time, like the weekend, when you can be more patient.

Get to the bottom of it. Find out what the problem is by letting your child wash their doll's hair in the bath – and see what it reveals. Often kids are afraid of the shampoo getting in their eyes or not being able to breathe, while others are afraid they will disappear down the plug-hole. Repeat what they are saying back to them so they know you have listened and understood, rather than dismissed their fears.

Let them help. When they are old enough, talk to them calmly at a time other than bathtime to talk through how to make it easier for them. Often they feel out of control. So asking them to pump out the shampoo or hold the shower-head during the rinsing may help.

Don't use too much water. It can be scary for a young child to have a jugful of water tipped over them or be approached with a high-power shower head. Instead, try using a thick sponge, which absorbs lots of water, and squeeze it gently over their head to get them used to the sensation. With a bit of practice, they might find they like the tickling feeling. Until they've only grown a bit of hair, this may be all it takes to rinse out baby shampoo. Use character gloves to make face-washing fun. Tell them Mr Monkey – or whoever – wants to kiss their face all over to get rid of the grime. Let their toys also help with hair-washing to keep the mood fun.

Give them something to look at. Take their mind off the process by sticking a plastic mirror at the end of the bath and use the shampoo foam to style their hair into mad styles – like a teddy bear's ears. Suggest they wash their toys' hair at the same time to give them something to focus on.

Use distraction. Stick funny pictures on the ceiling above the bath so they have something to focus on when they tip their heads back to get their hair rinsed. Sing a special hair-washing song so they know the process won't last long. Count down the rinses so they know the end is in sight.

Get in with them. The feeling of you supporting them will make them a lot more secure. Let them help wash your hair so it becomes more of a game. For children who feel unsafe in a big tub, try a bath ring, which will enable them to sit up – or a bucket-shaped wash pod. It will also free your arms to get the job done more efficiently.

Cut the steps. If you're on borrowed time, but your child's hair is a rat's nest, try a combined shampoo/conditioner followed by a spray de-tangler to cut the number of applications and rinses.

Set the water temperature. Save yourself the worry of little ones getting scorched by making sure your bathroom taps are set so they can't get too hot.

How to get kids to go to bed without a fuss

A word on sleep

More homework, packed extracurricular schedules, gadgets and waiting up late to see parents after work means that children are getting over an hour less sleep every night than they did a decade ago. But although their lives – and ours – may be becoming increasingly busy, youngsters still need as much rest as they ever did.

According to the NHS guidelines, children need 12 hours' sleep at the age of three, 11 hours at five and 10 hours at age nine. If they are not getting this, it makes your job much more difficult because over time, lack of sleep can have a serious impact on children's behaviour and mood. Among four-year-olds, one study of 9,000 kids who were short-changed on sleep 'externalised' their behaviour more – with more episodes of anger, overactivity, aggression and impulsivity.[21] The result is that mornings can become positively nightmarish because children are often irritable and disorganised.

Ironically, at the other end of the day, kids are no easier to put to bed at night because the hormone cortisol, which is released to keep them awake, also makes them wired. So even if they are exhausted, bedtimes become more fraught and ill-tempered too. In turn, you will be more stressed and tired trying to deal with them, setting up a true vicious circle.

You already know that a set bedtime is best, so stick to it – for your sake and theirs.

Be consistent

- Even if you are late home from work, don't expect the kids to wait up. Make up for it instead with a cuddle and a story in the morning. If you are often unable to get home in time to see the kids, look into flexible working – all UK parents are entitled to request it after six months in a job – or see if you can arrange to work a shift from home after they've gone to sleep. It's worth it to protect the most precious part of the day with your child.
- These days even quite young children have gadgets, like tablet computers, to play on. But in the run-up to

bedtime, the blue light that electronic equipment gives off suppresses the production of melatonin, the chemical that causes sleepiness. To make sure that children are tired in the evening, introduce 'a digital sunset' in your home, turning screens off at least an hour before bed. Think of it like giving kids too much sugar – you wouldn't give them a bagful of sweets at bedtime. As they get older, make sure all gadgets are removed from bedrooms, that they are only charged in communal areas and, if necessary, the broadband is turned off so they can't use devices under the covers.

- Unless they are trained, children do not recognise the signals that they are tired. Create an atmosphere in your home so that the importance of sleep is recognised by the whole family. Help them spot those signs that they will feel better if they get some sleep – like being tearful or easily frustrated. At calm times, explain to children that sleep is good because it helps them grow, learn new things and feel happier the next day, but don't make them anxious about it.

- Make bedtime a special time. Set aside this period to have some proper time with your children. Your child may well be happy to read to themselves by the age of eight or nine, but that doesn't mean you have to stop. By reading a bedtime story, you are sharing experiences and teaching them how to decipher the world. If you are exhausted after a day at work, let them read to you for a change – even if they are just making it up – or simply have a chat about how their day went.

- Don't pressure them. Repeatedly telling children to go to sleep and warning them they will be tired in the morning will only make them more anxious when they can't drop off. Instead tell them to relax – and reassure them that lying quietly in bed is almost as good as sleep.

How to stop technology stealing away time with your child

Children feel loved when we pay attention to them. They get the opposite message when we look more interested in checking our phones than looking at them. Don't make the mistake of thinking your children don't notice when your eyes flick down to your latest text, just because it's become normal or because they've given up complaining. If we only half listen and allow all our time to become enveloped by the creeping reach of technology, we risk losing our essential bond. The fact is that you can tell your child you love them a dozen times a day, but if you are texting and looking up at the clock as you do it, the message will be undermined. And what would you do if someone was usually looking the other way when you talked to them? You'd give up.

Your phone may have replaced your watch, your diary, your camera and your alarm clock. But here are some ways to prevent it replacing meaningful time with your kids.

- Be a good role model. Put away screens completely at meal times and at special times like bedtime.

- Think about the times your phone has caused upset in your home. Has your child tried to throw your phone down the loo? Do you notice them becoming more agitated and demanding when you are on it? Have you ever put their safety at risk by texting or talking on the phone while driving? Think of the bigger price you are paying for continuously checking it – and whether it's worth it. Ask yourself honestly: if your children were asked to describe your behaviour, would they mention that you often seem glued to a screen?

- Practise self-control when your phone rings or pings. Become conscious of how many times you are checking it and why – and what you are worried about missing out on. If you are home from work and spending time catching up with your children, turn off the sounds as they will make everyone tense. Try going 10, 20 and then 30 minutes at a time without checking it.

- Cut back on all your notifications and be brutal with spam. The only messages to make it to your phone should be important ones. Unsubscribe from non-essential mailing lists.

- If the answer to an email is likely to be more than 30 words, wait until you get to your computer, rather than becoming absorbed in it when you are supposed to be with your child. If it's important, it's likely you will write it faster and more coherently on a computer than a phone screen.

5 Happy holidaying:

travelling, birthdays and Christmas

Venturing further afield with children – sometimes even to the end of the road – can be a daunting prospect. And as they grow, keeping kids happy, well-fed and tidy when you are out and about takes the foresight of a seer and the patience of a saint. I have often marvelled at the amount of packing I have had to do to cover for every eventuality, just for a weekend stay with grandparents. So here are some steps to make it all that much easier.

Weekends away and holidays

Pack a laundry bag. Then you won't have the nasty job of weeding the dirty clothes from the unused stuff – and you can empty the bag into the washing machine as soon as you get home.

Take a dressing gown. When staying away, you don't want to be pulling towels around you so that you can leave your room to attend to a crying child. Take a dressing gown for an easy cover-up.

Stay coordinated. Pack all your children's clothes in the same range of colours. When you arrive, you'll be able to dress them more easily because everything will go together.

Don't fold, roll. Rolling clothes up is quicker and more space-efficient than folding.

Bundle outfits. Go one step further and roll together a complete outfit for each day – including pants and socks – in a freezer bag. It will save you time you would otherwise spend rummaging through your suitcase.

Use a crate. If the kids like to take a lot of bits and bobs, like favourite toys or books, when visiting relations for a few days, pop them in an open box or small crate, rather than trying to force everything in bags. This can work as a temporary toy box in the car and while you are away – and scooping everything up at the end of the visit will also be much quicker and easier.

How to make time in the car go faster

While some babies drop off to sleep as soon as they hear the hum of the engine, there are just as many who scream their heads off from the second you put your key in the ignition to the minute you pull up the handbrake.

And it doesn't get any easier as they get older. They just get better at asking for things.

The moment children are buckled in for a long journey, they quickly figure out it's not just them who's a captive. You are too.

Throw boredom and frustration into the mix and the result can be an endless catalogue of demands, many of which you are powerless to do anything about while you are on the road.

Few journeys will be entirely stress-free. But there are ways to make them pass more quickly – and with fewer infuriating 'Are we there yets?'

Every trip

- As soon as you open the car door, get into the habit of putting the keys straight in the ignition. After 10 minutes of buckling in, pacifying and loading up the boot, it's amazing how easily those keys can go astray, drop down the back of a seat or even fall into the gutter.
- Fit a sunshade in the rear windows. Remember that kids can't move freely in their seats, so it's hardly surprising if they are annoyed when the sun's shining in their eyes. Buy the type that can be pulled down like a blind.
- Keep a stash of loose change in the car. There's simply no such thing as just popping into a shop for change for the pay and display when you've got kids in tow. Spare yourself the stress, and build up a store of loose silver, but out of sight – it only takes a few pounds on view to tempt a thief to break in. Spend some calm time setting up automated payment services on your phone so you are not desperately trying to rig up accounts while you have a screaming baby in the back of the car and a traffic warden hovering.

Longer journeys

- Map reading is hard enough without adding kids, which is why almost all of us now have satellite navigation systems in our cars. But don't leave yourself entirely at the satnav's mercy. The Royal Society for the Prevention of Accidents suggests that all drivers take five minutes to look at the map before setting off to get a general idea of the route. This means that if you get distracted – or your child is screaming over the instructions – you still have a good general idea of where you're heading, and won't take that disastrous wrong turn on a major roundabout.

- Acknowledge how hard it is to be confined in a back seat for long periods. Plan ahead and check for parks and playgrounds en route so that children can let off steam on the way.
- Pack water bottles with sports tops as your refreshments. These are easy to open and close, and fit snugly into cup holders. If they spill, they don't leave a sticky mess – and the kids won't be on a sugar rush.
- Take easy snacks. Certain foods travel well when you're making long trips, like oatcakes and mini bagels, which are not so crumbly. Carrot sticks, and celery with peanut butter stay appetising all day and don't make too much mess. Although fiddly, pomegranate seeds and grapes cut in half are great thirst-quenchers too. On a hot day, keep your food cool by freezing drinks cartons to use as ice packs. If you want to avoid fights in the back seat, put each child's allocation in a grab bag with their name on it, so they don't row over who is hogging what.
- Get older kids involved by giving them their own map and marking the route with a pen. It gives them a sense of control over where they are going, and they can work out for themselves how far you've gone. Ask them to help navigate and look for interesting features along the way. Looking at the view – instead of trying to fix their focus – will also help keep travel sickness at bay.

- Use a shoe organiser with lots of compartments tied to the back of the seats in front to store a good selection of boredom-busting items for kids. Good ideas include a compass, binoculars, window wax crayons and stickers.
- Pack one towel in the back seat for every child. It can be used as a blanket, a mop for any spills, or on toddlers' laps to help toys stay put. You can also tuck one end into the window and hang it as a curtain to keep out the sun. If children get hot and sweaty, you can also moisten it with water to help keep them cool.
- For longer journeys, get a car seat with a clip-on tray so kids have somewhere to rest their toys. Swap children around in their seats to stop them getting bored.
- Even if you absolutely hate the thought of hypnotising your kids with screens, a long journey is probably the one time when it's in *your* best interests to make an exception. Remember, you need a break too – constantly having to turn round to cater to every whim is a painful experience.
- Take a pair of kitchen tongs in the car with you, to help retrieve the toy that someone's dropped, when it's just out of reach.
- If the repeated question 'Are we there yet?' is driving you to the limit, help kids realise how often they are saying it by taking a bag each of their favourite treats. Each time they ask, gobble one up – and tell them they will only get whatever's left at the end of the journey. It will make them think twice about repeating this refrain all through the journey.

What you really need in a car

A roadside assistance membership card. It really is an emergency when you've broken down and have young children with you. So make sure you've got a phone number and membership number at hand. When you are ferrying kids around, you will almost inevitably leave the lights on at least once, and need help with a flat battery.

Spare old scarves, hats and gloves. So you don't have to run back into the house at the last minute.

Umbrellas galore. Buy the broadest, toughest ones you can. Don't bother with kids' brollies until the age of about six. They don't really have the patience, control or strength to hold them up until then.

Pac-a-macs. Take loose fitting all-in-one macs with hoods, baggy enough to be pulled on over coats.

Sunscreen. Make application quick and easy by only buying the aerosol, transparent versions.

A first-aid kit. Be prepared with a kit containing bandages, a foil blanket, dressings, tape and, crucially, plasters. Hopefully you won't need it. But nothing proves to a wailing child with a minor scrape that you are taking him seriously more than a plaster.

Wellington boots in a shoe bag. So you can leave them to dry out in the car – and stop the caked-on mud crumbling everywhere when it hardens. By the way, for my money, the best way of cleaning wellies is a high-pressure hose in the garden.

A square holdall. Train kids to carry their own stuff, but also keep a holdall for those times when you haven't got eight arms to help them carry musical instruments, book bags, lunch boxes and sports outfits.

Extra nappies. Only for the first couple of years, obviously, but a secret stash in the boot will often come in useful, not least because when you are on the move, an open boot is the easiest place to discreetly change a baby. They are also handy for general mop-ups.

Wipes and tissues galore. Useful for anything from cleaning dirty faces to bottoms – and even giving the interior of the car a quick clean when you have a spare five minutes. Some hand-sanitising gel is always useful too.

Defroster and ice scraper. Frost can wreak havoc with your school run timetable. Make sure you are equipped with both for winter mornings.

Spare pens and pencils. For scribbling down shop phone numbers, and allowing older kids to start their homework in the back when you're waiting somewhere.

Balls and skipping ropes. Keep them ready so you are always prepared for the park.

A little swing-top rubbish bin. It doesn't take long for your car to become a pig-sty on wheels if the only place to put rubbish is the ashtray.

How to make time go faster on an airplane

If long car journeys can be challenging, at least the dramas are played out in the relative privacy of your vehicle. Take your children on a plane, and there are roughly 200 tutting strangers, praying that you and your family won't be sitting anywhere near them.

Ignore them, of course, but also be prepared – for your own sanity.

- Get young toddlers used to the idea of a holiday abroad by pretending to take little breaks beforehand to teach them what the journey will be like – and how you expect them to behave.
- It might be called a travel buggy, but it's the last thing you need at an airport. If your little one is still small enough, carry him in a sling so your hands are free. It will also be useful if you need to settle him up and down the narrow aisles of a plane.
- The most challenging moment of air travel has to be getting through security with children in tow. Remember, you could well be juggling armfuls of coats and hand luggage – and on top of that the whole family will have to take their shoes off. You will then have about 30 seconds to get them all back on again. So avoid lace-ups and choose slip-ons for you and your children. Arrive in plenty of time at security so you can afford to let anyone impatient or in a rush go ahead of you. Getting through this bit is hard enough without other passengers raising your stress levels before you've even embarked.
- Take as little liquid and baby food as possible through airport security if you don't want the stress of proving your baby food jars and bottles don't contain explosives. You will need to produce every single liquid to be inspected – so keep them all together in one container. Most major airports will have a good selection of shops on the other side to buy your supplies, but look at the airport's website first to check what will be available.

- Where possible, travel with baby-friendly airlines who provide warmed baby food on board – or make life really simple by mashing up whatever you get served on the plane with some milk.
- Look for direct or non-stop flights. They may cost more, but avoiding the stress of connecting journeys will be worth it. If you have to make a connection, consider making the change at smaller airports where you won't have to travel between terminals.
- Kids can get fidgety and bored in their seats before you even take off. So if you are travelling with a partner or friend, let them take advantage of the pre-board invitation, and load the hand luggage on while you keep the kids entertained at the gate, where they can run around until the last moment.
- Have a bottle – or breast – ready for take-off and landing because the sucking motion helps stop babies' sensitive middle ears from hurting and helps their ears pop.
- Before you take off, most stuff will need to be packed in the overhead locker, so keep a hard core of essentials – snacks that won't spoil, drinks, wipes and favourite toys – in a small bag that you can keep in the seat pocket in front of you.
- Take two or three favourite toys, plus a couple of novelties to keep kids amused – but don't take fiddly things like Lego or toy characters that will drop down the sides of the seats. Opt for larger all-in-one toys whose pieces don't fall apart – like scribble pads with attached pens – or you could always load some age-appropriate apps on your tablet. On flights, there is no denying that iPads can be a life-saver.
- Bring plenty of wipes. You can never have enough. Wipe down the seats beforehand to stop kids picking up germs.
- Don't scrimp on snacks. Never rely solely on airline food. If the wait for the drinks trolley seems a long time to you,

imagine what it's like for a toddler. Try to pack food that's not too crumbly, salty or likely to melt.

- As well as taking changes of clothes for the kids, dress in layers yourself so you can peel off to reveal a fresh, clean outfit underneath. Load up on disposable bibs for babies and toddlers so you are not carrying gloop-covered ones in your bag.

- As you can see, there is a lot to get ready if you don't want to be stuck high and dry without a vital item at 90,000 feet. So if you work, consider taking a day off before the holiday starts to get ready. You will kick off your break in a much more relaxed state.

Packing with kids

- With a million things to hold when you're travelling through an airport with a child, put all your travel documents in a big plastic purse (or small messenger bag across your chest) so you can find them instantly.

- Clothes and equipment can take up a lot of room – but at the same time you don't want to be lugging multiple suitcases. If you're staying with friends or relatives at the other end, pack clothes in a vacuum storage bag. When you suck the air out of it, you will have double the space. Repeat on the way back.

- If you pack really well, you may just manage to fit the whole family's needs into one case – which means less lugging and time waiting at the other end with tired children. To get the most in, fold T-shirts and shirts inside one another so they have fewer wrinkles (some packing experts recommend doing this around a rectangle of cardboard). They will also be ready sorted when you arrive. Instead of folding, roll the rest of your clothes into tight sausages.

Happy birthdays

Jelly, sandwiches, musical bumps and a slice of sponge cake wrapped in a napkin to take home. Do these simple childhood memories make you yearn for the days when children's birthdays were a bit less complicated?

Over the past few years, it seems that what used to be low-key celebrations have turned into major extravaganzas. With all the pressure to keep up, no wonder so many of us have more butterflies than Elton John's party planner when the time comes to think of what we are going to do for the next one.

But think again: are these events better – or just bigger? Instead of our kids having more fun, isn't the truth that these parties are becoming too fraught?

If we get stressed, our children feel that anxiety too – and that's no fun for anyone. The truth is that they will enjoy a party much more if it's not too overwhelming and it's pitched at just the right level for them. I don't know a child who wouldn't rather have their parent smiling and laughing alongside them than looking on anxiously from the sidelines.

How to have stress-free children's parties

Remember that with the best will in the world, your child won't actually have the best party if you are either running around like a headless chicken or barking orders like a professional events organiser. Here's how to throw a children's party that is less work and more fun – for everyone.

Don't overdo the guest list. If they are at school, don't feel you have to invite the whole class if you haven't got the space. The golden rule for a manageable number of guests is one per year of age of the child.

Ask them. As they get older, check with kids what *they* want. At the same time, think back to your best memories from your own childhood birthday parties. Were those golden moments about how much money your parents spent – or old-fashioned fun that cost nothing? Keep it in perspective.

Don't over-organise. Bear in mind that kids don't have to be directed the whole time to enjoy themselves. If you ask them, most often they will say they want a mad time with their closest friends – without too many rules. Chaos can be fun in itself. Remember, it's a celebration, not a school day.

Make it a team effort. Do you have a sibling or other relation who loves making cakes? Ask them to make one instead of giving a present. Do you have an artistic young cousin who could have a go at some simple face-painting? There are loads of tutorials for beginners on YouTube – as well as ideas for party games. Just be sure to make it a fun team effort, not a three-line whip.

Send e-invites and email thank-yous. There are some fantastic e-card party invites available on the web, which are just as fun as traditional cards and which take a fraction of the time to send. After the party, write down who gave what – and then email a brief thanks with a party picture attached.

Easy, cost-effective ways to decorate

Change the lighting. Nothing instantly transforms a boring room into a party venue as much as different lighting. There are so many reasonably priced sets available, ranging from themed fairy and lantern lights to lava lamps. Just be careful to place them securely and out of reach of kids, as they can get hot.

Inflatable fun. Balloons are old favourites, and again the choice has never been so varied. Carpet the floor with them so kids can run and jump through them and bat them at each other. If you are having your party at home, get ahead by blowing them up the night before.

Hang banners and bunting. Banners now come in lots of beautiful designs and stretch for metres, which means lots of decoration for your money. Bunting and pom-poms are also quick and easy ways to dress up a party venue.

Go one-stop shopping. The good news is that you can now buy ready-made party kits with matching bunting, cups and plates. Get more for your cash by signing up to voucher websites or schemes in the months before the party.

Forget party bags. They are an administrative nightmare. Instead go for party-themed gifts and hand them out as the kids are leaving.

Go outside. If you are holding a party in the summer, put up a wallpaper table outside and cover it with brown paper. Draw on place mats and place names with crayons – and let the children fill in the rest.

The best parties for every age

First birthday party. These parties are, let's face it, more about a picture opportunity and a slap on the back for making it through the first year than for your baby, who won't know what day it is. Babies can get over-stressed by too much noise and people, so keep it short and sweet and restrict it to one or two of your friends or close family members.

Age two to four. Little ones of this age are still learning what having a birthday party means, so keep it low-key and restrict the size of the guest list to your child's age, plus one. A simple theme is easiest in the early years – like water, sand or plasticine play.

Age five to six. When their child first starts Reception at five, many parents feel they have to invite the whole class, partly to be friendly and partly out of fear that their child might get left off a guest list at a later stage if they don't. Put your worries aside because having up to 30 kids is likely to turn into a major stress not only for you but also your child. For many children, play is very gender-based at this stage, so if you want to cut down numbers roughly along these lines, other parents are likely to understand. If you are still thinking of inviting a large group, make sure you don't leave out a proportion of less than half of the class. Otherwise kids are bound to find out – and could well feel excluded.

Age six to nine. By this age, children often have a theme in mind – sometimes based on a favourite movie or character. The result, not surprisingly, is that your daughter could end up being the third girl in the class to ask for a *Frozen* party – or your son the fourth to ask for a Spiderman do. If so, don't worry. In the words of a certain song: 'Let it go'. If that's what they are really into, make it happen. The good news is there many different ways to do the same idea. For a *Frozen* celebration, you could plan a karaoke event, an Elsa craft-making session, or a baking party to create frosty-looking cupcakes. For a Spiderman do, you could create a basic assault course in your garden to let guests show off their Spidey skills – or take a smaller group to a rock-climbing centre.

Age nine to 12. By around Year Four and Five, many children are in more defined friendship groups and starting to prefer smaller parties of no more than six or eight. Discretion is key here. At school, tell your child not to rub in the fact that they are having a celebration – and ask them to ask friends not to spread it around. Teach them empathy by explaining that others may feel hurt if they are not on the guest list.

As you see children increasingly affected by peer pressure, you may also worry that your child needs an even flashier party to keep up with classmates. First check if that's what they really want.

If they are asking for expensive gadgets as presents, explain that every family has a budget, and they can choose whether they would like the amount spent on the gift or the celebration with friends. Help make the cost real by translating the price of a super-extravagant party into the number of hours you would have to work to earn that money. Explain that there's only so much cash to go around and most of it needs to go on the day-to-day things that keep them healthy and comfortable. I don't know a child in the world who wouldn't want to see more of their parents rather than less, because they have to disappear off to work to pay for a super-expensive party.

Keep in mind that your children love you for how much you know and listen to them – not for how much cash you throw at a once-a-year event. Ultimately remember that a kid's birthday party can be child's play – as long as you keep it about the child.

More ways to make birthday preparations a bit easier

- **Buy a gift wrap holder.** Wrapping paper can be fiddly to store, so buy a special upright holder and also use it to keep ribbon, tape, bows and tags. Only buy sticky tape on a plastic roll with a dispenser so you are not always searching for the edge.

- **Bag it.** Better still, instead of wrapping up presents, buy a job lot of coloured paper gift bags (I often buy the cheap batches of brown paper ones or white ones on Amazon to last the whole year.) Just slip the gifts inside – and tie the handles together with ribbon.

- **Buy in bulk.** Don't go shopping every time your child has a party to go to. Snap up toys whenever you see them on sale, and bag them all in one go so there's never a last-minute panic. Some of the best deals are often from children's book clubs. For instance, one company recently offered all 15 Roald Dahl paperbacks for just £15.99 – a saving of nearly £70 – enough to keep a child's class in presents for the rest of the year. There was no membership fee and no postage and packing fees either. Or if you have not had time to buy something, email the parents an online gift voucher – or design and print one out in time for the party.

How to save time at Christmas

Get Santa to come to you. Avoid trudging into your local town centre and queuing for hours for the kids to see Santa by hiring your own to come to your house. A whole host of companies now offer personalised visits for as little as £15 per child. Allowing for the cost of travel and parking, it may work out cheaper and will certainly be more memorable.

Compile your Christmas list all year round. Does your mind go blank when the rest of the family ask what your kids want? When you're out shopping, take pictures on your phone to jog your memory – or keep an ongoing Pinterest board. Keep the brochures that drop through your door in the run-up to Christmas to remind you of what you would like, and tag pages with Post-it notes or by folding over the corners of the page.

Take advantage of gift-wrapping services. Some stores will either do it for you or provide you with the materials. One particularly busy year, I did my entire Christmas shop at IKEA and then took advantage of the reams of brown paper and sticky tape they have on hand near the delivery desk. When I got home, all I had to do was dress up my parcels with ribbon. You can sometimes pay a bit extra to get your gift sent directly from a website already wrapped.

Keep it plain. Use heavy-duty rolls of brown wrapping paper – not the flimsy, patterned stuff, which will leave you with lots of left-overs you can't do anything with. There's often more of it for less money, it's easy to control and stick down – and it can be dressed up any way you like.

Nail the Christmas lights. Taking the Christmas tree down may be one of the most depressing jobs of the year. Be better prepared for next year by wrapping the lights around a hanger, paper towel roll or piece of cardboard; and put your baubles in egg boxes to save the stress of untangling them when the kids can't wait to trim the tree again.

Christmas cards. There seem to be fewer and fewer cards each year – but if you still want to send personal cards, keep it simple. Log on to one of the websites where you can turn your favourite family pictures into postcards. On the other side, print a Christmas message. It will take about 10 minutes – and you won't need to stuff envelopes. Don't worry if you haven't written a personal message on each one. The fact that there's a special picture on the front will go a long way. Or buy animated personalised e-cards from companies like JibJab, which you can share with friends on social media.

How to have a calmer Christmas Day

Draw up a timetable and explain the plan. Put children in the picture by making it clear and talking through in advance what the plan is for Christmas Day. Don't let them rip every present open in the morning just after they've had their stockings. Try to leave opening gifts under the tree until the afternoon to give them an incentive to behave.

Stick to a routine. Over Christmas, visits to family and friends mean that the normal routines can often get forgotten. Stick to regular mealtimes and bedtimes as much as you can to avoid melt-downs. If you have friends and relatives staying, get them to pitch in by helping with bedtime and bathtime duties so that you are not handling childcare as well as entertaining.

Head off flashpoints. If children are likely to row over a new game, keep a timer handy so that there's no debate over how long a turn lasts. That way, everyone can see

---

that they are getting an equal go without the need for an argument.

Watch children's sugar levels on Christmas Day. If they're stuffing their faces with chocolate on an empty stomach as soon as they open their eyes in the morning, of course their blood sugar levels will be on a rollercoaster ride all day. So don't stuff stockings with sweet things that they will be gobbling from 6am onwards – fill them instead with non-edible treats.

Keep it in perspective. The more parents give, the more kids expect. So don't fall into the trap in the run-up to Christmas of continuously buying because you think you've never got enough. In a year's time, the children probably won't even remember what they got – but you will be left with a large credit card bill which may mean you have to work harder and spend less time with them afterwards. Remember, the ultimate gift for any child is a happier, less over-worked you.

 6 Housework hacks:

shortcuts to speed up the chores

The American humourist Erma Bombeck once wrote: 'Cleaning your house with kids around is like shovelling the sidewalk before it's stopped snowing.' Now, I've never cleared a pavement in a blizzard, but I know exactly what she means. Trying to keep the house under control with children around is a relentless, and often thankless, task. As soon as you've got one spadeful out of the way, there's more to pick up.

It's rather an outdated idea in the 21st century, but for some reason many women still feel that keeping the house under control is mainly their responsibility. But don't forget that your children need you more than your shelves need dusting. As long as it's safe and reasonably organised, your home doesn't need to be as spotless as a show home. Change your viewpoint. Look on tidying as a way to make your life easier and get things done more smoothly.

How to keep your house under control in less time

Choose wipe-clean paint. There are few things that prove more definitively that you have given up on your home than kiddy handprints left all over the wall. It feels like it's all downhill from there. So choose gloss or wipe-clean paint so you can clean them off speedily. It sounds paradoxical, but white is the easiest colour – because you can touch it up more easily when the paintwork gets chipped.

Fit dimmer switches. Change the mood in an instant by turning down the lights at the end of the day. Low lighting will also camouflage the worst of the remaining mess.

Think hardwood or laminate flooring. It's easier and won't stain. Having washable rugs instead of fitted carpets will make cleaning more manageable.

Ban ornaments. Avoid trinkets around your living area as much as possible. They are dust magnets that are fiddly to clean and easy for kids to break. Focus on larger items in your living room, and leave it at that.

Get practical photo frames. Never buy frames that need to have the back unscrewed to replace the picture. Kids grow quickly, and by the time you've got round to finding the right screwdriver, the baby in the picture frame could easily be in secondary school. Choose frames where you can simply slide the pictures in and out. Also avoid silver or brass frames unless you want to add polishing off metal tarnish to your to-do list.

Designate a play area. Even if you don't have much room, find a space in your living area that's just for your kids. Make a child-size table the hub and install a toy box nearby. Make it their own separate area that doesn't need clearing away for meals or any other activities. Screen it off after children have gone to bed if necessary.

Be generous with waste bins. Every room should have one to keep them tidy. Forget wicker or leather. A funky moulded design is the most practical, as children's bins in particular will need a good wash in the dishwasher now and then.

Cover your sofa. Get a washable throw for your sofa in a fabric that can be chucked in the washing machine the moment it gets soiled. Again, it sounds counter-intuitive, but white is the best colour – simply because you can pop it in the washing machine and bleach out any stains.

Ditch the pot plants. I can't remember the last time I went to someone's home and came away thinking how lovely the plant in the corner looked. Generally they are droopy-looking dust magnets that also shed leaves. You've got enough to look after. Don't make more dusting, watering and vacuuming work for yourself.

Other ways to keep your home under control

- Tidy up as you go along. Do a quick scan of every room as you leave it to see if there's something you can take and put back in its proper place. Is there a water glass on the bedside table you could deliver to the kitchen now you are heading down there to make the kids' breakfast?

Does your child's favourite soft toy really belong on your bedroom floor – or should it go back on his bed on the way back to the kitchen?

- The fewer possessions you own, the less clutter you have, and the fewer things you have to care for and clean up after. Simplify your life and get rid of anything that's broken, that you don't like or don't use. As Victorian designer William Morris said: 'Have nothing in your house that you do not know to be useful or believe to be beautiful.'

Hallways

A disorganised hallway can mean serious delays leaving the house with children. And after a long day, coming back to a home where you have to fight your way through piles of discarded shoes and bags can be soul-destroying. Here's how to have a hallway that will guarantee you smooth exits – and make you glad to be back.

- Kids dumping coats and shoes the moment they walk in the door is the single biggest cause of disheartening pile-ups. It's essential to have enough hooks – including some placed at their level, so that they can hang their things up themselves, as they do at school. Give as much space to pegs as possible so coats don't knock each other off. A family of four will need eight hooks at the very least.
- If you have room, put a shoe cupboard in your entrance way for an instant make-over – you will no longer have to dash around the house to find the right pair. Get kids into the habit of depositing their footwear as soon as they come in and changing into slippers. Or consider a second coat hook rack at ground level where you hang shoes off the floor in easy pairs.

- Keep two doormats, one for outside the door and the other for inside. They will cut the amount of dust that comes into the house by up to 80% – and slash the time you spend vacuuming and sweeping.
- When the weather turns colder, put out a separate basket for each member of the family to deposit gloves, scarves and hats so they don't get mixed up.
- As soon as winter is over, take heavy coats out of circulation and store away out of sight.
- Get a mirror in the hallway – to give you the confidence to know you've got it together as you walk out the door. It will also make the children more likely to take some pride in their appearance, and put their coats on properly.

Bathroom

How to head off mess

- Forget soap bars. Buy push-down dispensers of foam soap because, unlike the gloopy liquid kind which kids will play havoc with, they dispense only a little at a time.
- Buy flip-top toothpaste so you are not constantly replacing the lids the children have left off.
- Order shampoos and conditioners in one-litre bottles online. They will cause less clutter and often come with a pump, making them easier to dispense.
- Invest in a toothbrush holder, and get children into the habit of putting theirs back straight away. Otherwise they will get lost in the bottom of mildewy cups or tangled up on the side of the basin.

How to clean the bathroom more quickly

- Keep job lots of cleaning wipes – and other basic cleaning products – in the bathroom so you can give the toilet, sink, bath and floor a quick once-over whenever you have a spare minute. Also have a squeegee you would usually use for windows handy to clean the shower door fast.
- If your kids are old enough not to need you right next to them when they're in the bath, use the time to clean up sinks and loos. The steam will make it easier to wipe dirt and dried-up toothpaste off surfaces.
- To avoid empty toilet rolls cluttering up the bathroom, choose a holder which does not need to be unscrewed every time to replace one. Instead opt for the simple rod kind that allows you to slip the roll easily on or off.
- You will find the toothpaste stains left on the sink won't be quite as unsightly if you choose all-white brands, rather than ones with green and red stripes.

Keeping kids' rooms tidy

A child's room is their universe, and their most secure place in the world. By showing you care about what they think and making them responsible for it, they're likely to be more interested in keeping their environment tidy. Don't be put off organising your child's room because you don't have the time. A few hours of work will pay off further down the line, not least because you won't need to nag them so much about keeping it under control.

- Small children like to express their independence by being able to access items and later put them away on their own. So fit low shelves in alcoves. They store more than shelf units because they make better use of the space.

- Get a big basket for stuffed toys. Everyone always ends up with loads, but it's rare that any more than two or three are in favour at any one time. Don't allow them to take up space around a child's room unless they are very special to them.
- Keep a spare packet of wipes and paper towels in play areas. An extra dustpan and brush – or, even better, a hand-held vacuum – is always useful for picking up paper scraps and other debris.
- Stay away from wallpaper, unless you enjoy spending time redecorating, because children love ripping bits off it. It will also date. Instead use basic, neutral colours on the walls applied with wipe-clean paint. You can change the look of the room with wall stickers and new pictures as your child grows.
- Install a laundry basket so clothes have somewhere to go right away and don't end up on the floor.
- Put shoe boxes without lids in drawers to keep clothes from getting jumbled – put socks in one shoe box, pants in the next.

How to get kids to help

Training children to tidy up after themselves is a win–win situation: you get some help around the house, and it teaches them organisational skills and respect for others that will last a lifetime.

- Praise younger children for trying – not for results. At this stage, you are getting them to feel good about tidying up – not to work as industrial cleaners – and they are often more than happy to be mummy or daddy's little helpers.
- With older children, don't march into their rooms and shout 'Tidy your room!' or they'll just switch off. Instead

get them on the way by setting specific tasks, like picking up clothes and making the bed. Make it feel more fun and manageable by giving them a 10-minute time limit – and let them do it to music if it moves them along.

- If kids share rooms, stop blame games about who didn't put away what by colour-coding property with stickers. Mark each child's own space with rugs and use barriers, like book cases, to give them privacy.
- Give children a fighting chance by allocating a place for everything.Use tie racks for hair accessories, ice cube trays for marble and shell collections and cutlery trays and tool boxes for pens and paints. If they have been warned about leaving clothes on the floor, collect them up in a rubbish bag until they earn them back.
- Teach them how: start by investing time in showing your child how you want a task done. If you're going to ask a teenager to do laundry, make sure they know how to separate colours. Don't be put off if your child makes a pig's ear of it because they're little – or trying to discourage you from asking again.
- Create team spirit: see the family as a team where everyone helps create a home that's nicer to live in. Kids will often try to argue, 'I didn't leave that there.' Point out that you're all there to help each other.

Staying on top of paperwork

- Share your diary electronically with your partner so that you are always on the same page. Set up a shared contacts list too so you have the same access to important phone numbers and addresses. School emails should come to you both and you should both be equally able to arrange play-dates, social events and childcare.

- Keep work stuff away from home stuff. Permission forms for a school trip next week shouldn't get stuck among the tax forms you don't need to look at until next year. Sign school paperwork as soon as you get it and put it straight back in your child's book bag to avoid frantic searches on school mornings.
- Avoid allowing paperwork to build up because you are worried it's not safe to throw it in the bin. Take a pair of scissors to any address and account details, destroy and throw straight in the bin. Or keep a hand-held shredder – safely out of reach – close to where you go through your mail.
- Use plain postcards as birthday cards or thank-you notes. You won't have to address and stuff envelopes – and, even better, you won't have to dream up loads of things to write because there's so little space.
- Only touch each piece of paper once. Try to deal with it then and there.
- When you get the chance, make copies of important documents, like passports and birth certificates, and store pictures on your phone.
- Keep a secret set of spare keys for those days when you really can't find them in the rush. Also give a set to a trusted neighbour or friend who lives nearby. With so many things to think about when you leave the house with children, it's highly likely that one day you will dash off and lock yourself out.
- Make friends with your postman (or woman) and regular delivery staff. In these days of internet shopping, they are your interface with the outside world when it's tough to get to the shops. There's nothing more irritating than narrowly missing a drop-off – and then having to trudge to the post office collection point and stand in a queue to collect your package. Explain that it also might take you

longer to get to the door sometimes because you've got kids – and ask them to ring a couple of times before they give up if it's a delivery that needs a signature. Point out the safest place to leave an item if they don't get an answer.

- To track packages really quickly, just type the tracking number into Google and it should come up. Think about getting a phone app that tracks them automatically and sends you updates about when deliveries will arrive.
- If you're working on your laptop around kids, put your computer on a book or a slightly higher surface in case the children knock any liquid over, to give you a few seconds' grace.
- Keep a master to-do list: when your head is spinning in every direction, it's essential that you write down what needs to be done. Keep it going on your phone so you can add to it wherever you are.
- Organise everything you save to the computer to do with the children with the word 'KIDS' or your child's name first in the catch-line, so you don't have to fish around for documents.

Things you can never have too many of

Baby wipes

Batteries

Blu Tack/White Tack

Household cleaning wipes

Rolls of sticky tape and gaffer tape with dispensers

Scissors

Stamps

Tape measures (for internet shopping)

Ziploc bags

7

Looking after you:

tips to look good, feel good and de-stress

There was a time when as soon as you had kids, you could stop bothering about the way you looked. However, times have moved on, and these days there is the expectation – from both others and ourselves – that we should look just as good as we did before. And without the hours in the day to do it.

Of course, no one says you can't relax your standards, especially when you've recently had a baby. But when you do want to take some time over your appearance, here's how to reclaim yourself – but in half the time. By simplifying your regime, you will probably spend less too.

How to do your make-up more quickly

Buy make-up that does more than one job. Look for products that do two or even three things at the same time. For example, buy mascara that both curls and lengthens. Or try blushers that double as lip glosses, and combined foundation and powder compacts.

Cut out the middleman. Once upon a time, you probably had a vast array of make-up brushes for every conceivable job. Now you don't have the time to find them, let alone wash them. So choose make-up with built-in applicators, like lip gloss and concealer pens. Easier still, plump for make-up you can put on with your fingers, like tinted moisturisers and cream blushes, which are more natural looking anyway.

Use a make-up primer. It may sound strange to add one extra step before you've even started, but use a primer. It's quick, fills in surface imperfections like large pores and lines – and you can apply it without looking in the mirror (always a good test of a mum-friendly make-up technique). Primer's job is also to help make-up last, so you will look more polished for longer in the day.

If in doubt, chuck it out. Life is so much simpler when you edit out the stuff you don't need. It doesn't matter what brand it is, having make-up you don't use hanging around is a waste of time. Apply the wardrobe rule. If you haven't worn it for a year, bin it. Or ask yourself, if you were at the shops, would you buy it again? As much as it may break your heart, also throw out any cosmetics with broken packaging or missing lids. They're bound to cause an almighty mess further down the line.

Keep two sets of make-up. Put a spare set for touch-ups in your handbag, in a see-through bag so you can see what's in there and get to it fast. Then leave it there – never to be removed. At the very least, make sure you keep a combination rouge/lip gloss in your purse to revive you in times of need.

Do your make-up on the move. Get a professional make-up artist's make-up box to help keep it organised. Take it wherever your kids are. If they are happy playing with blocks in the playroom, take your kit there too – and you may get time to mascara a few extra lashes.

Save the bigger grooming jobs for night-time. The mornings are hectic enough, so just keep them for make-up. When the kids have gone to bed, take time to bleach your moustache, paint your nails or pluck your eyebrows. Or take advantage of bathtime with the kids and put on a mud mask.

Buy make-up that looks after itself. Wind-up pencil applicators aren't great value for money, because there's not much product in there. But there is nothing more irritating than not being able to find a liner with a sharp tip at the bottom of your make-up bag. So on this occasion, choose convenience over price.

Think about packaging. When you are looking for moisturisers and foundations, search out products that are easily dispensable, either by pumps or aerosols, rather than jars or tubes. That way, it won't be quite such a disaster if you can't find the top – and they are less likely to dry up or spill.

Choose a tinted moisturiser over foundation. Tinted moisturiser like BB cream is another of those beauty aids that passes the big test of easy mummy make-up. This does three things at once – gives coverage, moisturises and usually offers sun protection. Plus it can quickly and easily be applied with your fingers.

Go for shades as close as possible to your natural colours. When you are trying to look good in the minimum time, don't experiment. Bright tones will only underline the fact that you could do with some more sleep. Applying a statement shade of deep scarlet lipstick is going to take an awful lot more time and concentration than a subtle lip tint close to your own lip colour.

Eye whitener/redness eye drops. After working late or a sleepless night, this is the ultimate secret for the sleep-deprived parent. You will look as fresh as a daisy – even before you've applied a scrap of make-up.

Nail shortcuts. As with make-up, try to stick to a colour close to your natural shade, so your nails don't look so bad when they get chipped. Or forget the nail polish and just keep them short, clean and nicely rounded.

Stick it on the wall. The easiest way to have the basics at your fingertips is to stick them with some Blu Tack to the wall next to your dressing table mirror, so that you don't need to rummage around in drawers. I stick small flat pots of concealer, blush and lip gloss to the wall for instant access. Also keep a magnet on the wall to hold must-haves like tweezers, nail scissors, safety pins, plus a needle and thread for emergency clothes repairs. Keep a bin close for old cotton tips, packaging and make-up wipes.

Essentials for a faster make-up bag

- Primer to even out skin tone and keep your make-up on for longer
- Tinted moisturiser with built-in sun-screen
- Self-curling mascara
- Cream blush
- A self-sharpening eye pencil
- A lip tint close to your natural lip colour
- A generously sized make-up mirror which you can find easily
- A pan stick foundation/concealer – this type of coverage will help speed things up and can be used to cover uneven patches, shadows and eye-bags when you're in a rush

The 90-second make-up routine

1. Rather than using a liquid foundation, save time by using a tinted moisturiser you can apply with your fingers. Time spent: 10 seconds.

2. Instead of using brushes, use a cheek/lip colour you can also put on with your fingers. Then keep the product on standby to use on your lips for a more coordinated look. Time spent: 10 seconds.

3. Use a concealer to correct imperfections and as an eye base to open up your eyes. The pan stick versions are great because they can also fix under-eye bags and smooth out your complexion if you need more coverage. Time spent: 20 seconds.

4. Use a mascara that also curls, for example Maybelline Wonder Curl. Time spent: 30 seconds.

5. Apply your lip/cheek tint to your mouth. Time spent: 10 seconds.

6. Blot out any shine with powder. Time spent: 10 seconds.

Things to do now that will save you time in the long run

Dye your eyelashes. This is a brilliant thing to do about once a month. Waking up and looking like you already have mascara on gives you an instant lift – and saves so much time applying and removing the real thing.

Get your eyebrows shaped. Stop wasting time trying to get it right. Go to a professional to get the right basic shape. It will take 10 minutes. It's the easiest way to make your face look groomed without any make-up.

Rinse your hair in cool water. Hate the bird's nest look when you get out of the shower? For the last two minutes let the water run cool so that the hair cuticles close up again. Your hair will be easier to comb through and shinier.

Sleep with your conditioner. Go to bed slathered in the stuff and covered with a shower cap. Your hair will be healthier, less frizzy and easier to style for the whole week.

Mix your products. Blend your sunscreen with your moisturiser, or your exfoliator with your cleanser and get the job done in half the time.

Keep spare packets of make-up wipes. Keep a packet of wipes for dealing with spills, cleaning up dispensers or freshening up your face before touch-ups. I keep some in the car to take off my make-up on the way back from evenings out when I want to go straight to bed.

If you haven't got any time at all . . .

Wear sunglasses. They hide bags and can make you feel glamorous on the most unglamorous of days.

High pony tail/bun. Give it a little height and bounce – and you can look instantaneously chic.

Your hair

Hair is probably the hardest beauty task-master of all for a busy mother. Take another look at how you are handling the big three Cs – condition, colour and cut – and you may find ways to spend less time dealing with it.

Condition

Whatever your hair is like, try to cut back on the blow-dry habit. Maybe you are caught in a vicious circle. In an effort to get the job done quickly, you dry your hair on the high heat setting, so your hair becomes dryer and frizzier. You then have to blow-dry it even more to tame it.

But if you take a few steps to get your locks back in condition, you will be able to wean yourself off this particularly time-draining habit.

Cut

Some mums do it, but I don't think it's realistic for a woman who likes having long hair to cut it off because they now have kids. In fact, shorter hair styles can end up being higher maintenance because you will need more visits to the salon to keep the shape.

The beauty of long hair is that you can quickly throw it back into a pony tail or have it half-up and half-down.

But first ask your stylist to give you a cut that suits your hair, works with the texture, and will take the minimum blow-drying to maintain (or better yet, if you are lucky, none!).

Colour

Try to wean yourself off the hair dye. Stay within two shades of your natural colour to ward off obvious roots and stave off time between visits to the salon. You may be surprised by how much better you look when your hair is matched to your natural skin tone.

If you can't let go of your trademark look, one of the best ways to keep hair colour looking better for longer is to protect it by staying out of the sun. As your hair is exposed to sunlight, the protein structure in it becomes oxidised and permanently broken down by the UV rays, changing the tone and gradually making it a lighter shade. Highlighted hair is already damaged, so UV rays will make that worse.

Another key way to prolong your colour is to protect it when you swim in a pool. It's actually not the chlorine in the water that turns hair green, it's the copper. To avoid getting this greenish tint, wear a swimming cap, or use a waterproof protective hair product.

Hair shortcuts

Get the right equipment. You will save hours of your life if you simply invest in a professional-strength hairdryer. True, it will be twice the cost of a cheap domestic one, but it can cut the drying time by at least half because they come with higher voltage and make this often tortuous process so much more efficient. Look for models which come with a 'cold shot button' to give a blast of cold air that seals in your style at the end. Just by using the nozzle attachments and drying downwards, you hair will also dry more smoothly and with less frizz. Professional hairdryers also tend to come with longer, more flexible cables for salon use, so you can dry your hair wherever the kids are, if needs be. If you straighten your hair, only straighten the essentials – like your fringe or the bits closest to your face.

Leave out the conditioner. Avoid using moisturising conditioners if you are in a rush because your hair will take longer to dry afterwards. That's because these products coat the hair in a water-resistant film. When time is really at a premium, don't condition. Instead, detangle when you get out of the shower with a spray-on, leave-in version.

Get speedy products. Check out products, like quick blow-drying spray, which promise to speed up the process and give heat protection from your blow-dryer at the same time. If you've got short hair, go for the messy look and invest in some good hair products that will keep your hair styled all day.

Dry shampoo. These products have staged a dramatic comeback in the last couple of years. Keep a can on hand for those days when you know you won't have time to wash your hair. For better results, put it in a plait and then into a bun. When you undo it the next day, the wave and body should have returned to your mane. Then tip your head upside down and spray the crown with a dry shampoo to create a mass of loose waves. Just don't overdo it or you'll look like you've gone grey.

How to blow-dry your hair faster

- Towel dry your hair (or, better yet, use a wrap-up turban, which dries it more quickly and allows you to do other stuff instead of balancing a towel on your head) so it's about 80% dry.

- After applying hair products to speed up the process, tip your head over and then to each side, and blow-dry from above on a medium setting in the direction of growth, so you don't ruffle up the cuticles and make the hair frizzy.

- Keep running your fingers through your hair and lifting it from the roots so that the air circulates through and it dries faster. When the hair is ready to style, use a vented hair brush for the same reason. Look for the model with the biggest head so that you can style larger sections at a time.

- Now you are ready to do the finishing touches, fix the nozzle to the end to direct the air flow downwards again to make the surface of the hair smooth.

- Target the most obvious sections: if you literally only have a few minutes, dry only the top and the front. Start at the crown so you are not brushing moisture down into the rest of your hair. Then concentrate on the bits at the front – which is what people look at.

- Finally seal the style with a blast of cold air, which will make the hair shafts contract, and set it in place.

How to wake up looking better

When you are juggling a lot of balls, and surviving on not very much sleep, there will no doubt be mornings when you are almost too afraid to look in the mirror. We've all been there. But there are some things that can help you jump out of bed looking almost ready for the day. Best of all, you can do some of them last thing at night, when you finally have some time to yourself.

- Put your hair in a ponytail or loose plait when you go to bed. Then it will stand a better chance of looking reasonably unruffled and knot-free in the morning.
- Apply fake tan last thing at night with your moisturiser – whatever the weather. You will wake up looking healthy and glowing – and need loads less make-up.
- Make sure you take off all your eye make-up before bed (it's worth getting a good waterproof eye make-up remover to get the job done faster) so your eyes aren't blood-shot or irritated by debris that builds up overnight.
- Dye your eyelashes at home when the kids are asleep so you won't need mascara when you wake up. Use eye drops to get any redness out the next morning.
- In the morning, use your fingertips to massage your skin just under your jaw line and around your eye sockets and hairline to improve blood circulation to the face and boost lymphatic drainage to remove toxins. Splash your face in a sink of ice-cold water to get your glow back.

How to get dressed in two minutes instead of 10

There will be some days when you have literally five seconds – at most – to get dressed. Here's all you need to know about looking together – but in a fraction of the time.

Get your colours done. Deciding what to wear is much easier if you know what definitely suits you. Take the guess-work – and the tangerine and lilac wardrobe mistakes – out of your wardrobe by finding out what the best tones are for you. When you actually know for certain what colours work with your hair and skin, you will instantly be able to identify the items that make you look your best. Eventually you will also build a wardrobe of matching colours that will take the time-wasting indecision out of dressing in the morning. You will also be able to shop faster online because you will be able to search more quickly for the shades you know work for you. These days you don't have to see a consultant to work out what shades suit you best. There are online quizzes to help guide you – search for 'colour analysis'.

Get out a tape measure. We all know that clothes sizes vary wildly between stores. Do you actually know what your measurements are, or do you usually make an educated guess? When you're shopping online, be equipped with all your vital stats – including the length of your legs – to avoid returning items that don't quite fit. Or keep a tape measure close at hand.

Check it out online first. If it's an emergency and you have to head for the high street, spend half an hour browsing through the collections online beforehand so you have a good overview of what's out there. If you are not confident in putting together outfits, take a shortcut by signing up to free styling websites like getmystylist.com and mystylit.com. These assemble outfits from current collections in the shops based on your shape, the parts of your body you want to show off or play down, and your budget. They make money if you click on the suggested items of clothing and buy them. But even if you don't purchase anything, you are still getting plenty of free ideas on how to coordinate the latest outfits in ways that will suit your body shape.

Invest in good underwear. If you have greying bra straps, droopy bras that have lost their lift, saggy pants or underwear that can be seen when it's not meant to be, then you will look – and feel – like a slob. Get your bust size measured, in case it's changed since having children, then re-stock. If you are very active with your kids, invest in a range of comfortable sports bras with strong support so you are ready to run around after them.

Find the perfect dress shape for you. Find a style that flatters. Then look for it in materials that wash well. Beware of too many zips and buttons. If possible, an easy dress should slide over the head in one smooth move. When you're trying it on, don't just judge it on how it looks. Time how long it takes to put on – and consider whether it will need ironing.

Make it easy. Forget the clothes that need special care or are dry clean only. Say goodbye to silk, sequins, beads, bows that untie and the rest. Resist bell sleeves, ribbons or ties that will end up trailing in all sorts of unspeakable substances. Steer clear of stripes or spots. Bold prints will be impossible to match with tights and other accessories in a rush.

Layer it. Wear layers you can peel off as they get progressively covered in sick, paint, baby food, etc.

Buy longer tops. Unless you are very lucky, your tummy probably isn't as flat as it used to be. So dump short tops. There's nothing more uncomfortable than continually tugging them down over a bulging stomach.

Top wardrobe tips

- If you have the room, hanging is easier than folding and you can see what you've got more easily. It's also easier and quicker to hang on hooks than arrange on a hanger. Use a tie rack for hanging your camisole tops or slips so you can find them without rummaging.

- Throw out wire hangers as soon as they enter your house. You will only end up wrestling with them when they get tangled up. Instead, invest in decent wooden hangers with rubber ends or clips so you are not constantly re-hanging clothes that have slipped off.

- You won't be going anywhere, I hope, without your underwear. Yet there have been many times when I have been hunting around in the tangled mess of tights, belts and bras to find a pair of pants in the morning. Use shoe boxes to divide your drawers into compartments.

- Keep your tights separate from your socks and as soon as the weather is warm enough, banish them from your sight before they create any more chaos.

- To save the frustration, keep an 'odd sock drawer' for the whole family, where odd socks can be reunited.

- Hang your scarves and shawls from hangers – you can see them better and they won't get so creased.

Your school run essentials

The useful school run wardrobe

- A good well-made darker-coloured coat (see below)
- A mac with a hood for rainy days
- A pair of black leggings or jeggings to wear with baggy knits and under dresses
- A black polo neck jumper to wear with jeans and under dresses
- Your signature dress in several different textiles and colours
- A bad-hair-day hat
- A set of black and white long-sleeved T-shirts to go under tops and take dresses from summer to winter
- A pair of boots with a solid heel
- A pair of trainers
- A pair of ballet flats

The useful school run coat

Because of the vagaries of the British weather, your coat is always going to be a key item in your wardrobe, so it's important to get it right. A good one will also hide all manner of sins underneath – including the dreaded pyjamas if necessary – and still make you look pulled together.

- Look for a dark, plain colour – preferably black, brown, grey or navy – that will wear well and won't need repeated dry cleaning. If it sounds dull, you can always accessorise or brighten up with scarves if you get a spare minute.
- Choose a smart but not too tight shape so that it can be slipped over most things without a struggle but doesn't

look like a shapeless sack either. A-line or a mannish overcoat style often works well.

- If your style will allow it, look for a coat with a hood. It will mean you won't need an umbrella when it's raining – and will have both hands for the kids.
- Consider buying one with large square pockets that will carry all manner of things from snacks to baby bottles and, of course, your keys and phone. A good-sized pair of secure pockets will also give you the freedom to leave the house without a handbag if you're in a real rush. Beware of pokey triangular pockets. Everything will just fall out before you've even realised it.

The easiest handbags

A good handbag is the mother ship of the busy mum's life. Getting it organised can mean the difference between feeling prepared to face the world and scarcely daring to leave the house. So look for the following features.

- Get a size that's not so small that it's constantly overflowing, but not so big that you need wheels to pull it along.
- Avoid bags in soft pale materials that stain easily. Instead opt for darker, harder materials – or even wipe-clean patent.
- When you are shopping for a new bag, try it with the coat you will usually wear it with so you know it will fit comfortably over your arm. For summer, make sure the material is not too hard against bare skin.
- Make sure that when you put the bag down, it stands up. The last thing you want is to put it down and have the entire contents spill out on the floor.

- Check it's got the right number of compartments and outer pockets that close securely. It should have sections for your purse, mobile phone, key, lipsticks and sunglasses – and if possible something at the end to hold a bottle or beaker upright. Don't overdo it, though. I once bought a bag with five pockets on each side. Finding my mobile was like playing treasure hunt.
- Instead of a classic bucket-style handbag, think about swapping for a smarter version of a back-pack style, which will leave you hands-free to tend to the kids and push a stroller.

And how to manage the contents

- You are going to need to fit everything in it, bar the kitchen sink, so shrink everything down. Buy a mini-size brush and travel-size versions of your favourite make-up.
- Do you feel that you are constantly fishing around in your bag for your mobile, which only rings for five seconds before it goes to voicemail? Call your phone company to get them to extend the ring tone remotely or search online for the codes which will make it keep going for at least a good 30 seconds or more before it cuts off. On this subject, always set up the 'find my phone' feature because when you are distracted with children, it's likely to get lost or mislaid.
- Get into the habit of always putting your mobile in the same zippable outer pocket every time, so you are not constantly rooting around in a panic for it. Keep it away from anything wet if you want it to survive.
- Keep nappies and wipes in separate Ziploc bags. Otherwise the wipes will either dry up or leak – and nappies swell up when they get moist.
- Only keep ballpoint pens in your bag, preferably washable ones with the lids on so you don't get scribbles on the

inside. Pencil leads will break. Felt-tip or roller ball pens will at some point meet with your baby wipes or bottle and start a nightmarish chromatology experiment.

- Buy the most substantial key ring you can find to make keys harder to lose. Don't bother with the type that beeps when you whistle. I thought they would change my life, only to find out the alarm was set off by every screech and cry. Instead consider using a rock climbing-type clip to attach your keys to your bag handle so you can always fish them out from the depths. Some handbags will come with these built in.
- Never be tempted – even in a hurried moment – to put any food in your bag unless it's in some sort of Tupperware container. Otherwise you will soon end up fishing out oatcake fragments, squashed satsumas – and much worse. Even the firmest, ripest banana can cause havoc in seconds if it's forgotten in the bottom of a handbag.
- When it comes to your period, don't put paper-wrapped applicator tampons in your bag. Inevitably they will come into contact with some sort of wetness, swell up and burst out of the wrapper, making them unusable. By comparison, the bullet-shaped plastic-covered ones stay dry and are more compact.
- Keep your extra set of make-up (remember your duplicate set that you supposedly never touch?) in a tough clear plastic bag with good zips, like the ones they sell in airports. That way you will be able to see the product you need instantly, rather than having to root around for it.
- If you are out and about with your child, take some entertainment other than your smartphone. Buy everything in miniature – mini colouring books, pencil sets and even tiny plastic doodle pads. They don't take up much room, but on a trip out of the house they can make all the difference.

Eating healthily

As every parent knows, there are far more sweet temptations around when you have kids.

With the kitchen cupboard and fridge packed with treats for your little ones, chocolates, crisps and ice-cream can be simply too good to resist.

That's not the only danger.

More than six out of 10 mums say their body image has got worse since they had children.[22] And according to researchers at the University of Chicago, a year after giving birth nearly 75% of women believe they are in worse shape than they were before they had their child.[23] So here are some tips and tricks to help busy parents stay in shape.

- Start the day with an egg. The protein boost will keep you – and the kids – fuller for longer. Most children love them boiled – and make it fun by giving them a crayon to draw on funny faces before they eat them. Keep up your protein levels throughout the day – by grabbing a handful of nuts, for example – to keep your blood sugar levels stable through the day.
- Never let your children hear you obsessing about weight or food – and do not use the word 'diet' around them. You will pass on negative body messages. In any case, the goal, if the subject comes up, should be a balanced sense of health and fitness.
- Resist the temptation to finish off the kids' leftovers at teatime. As soon as they've finished, throw the remnants straight in the bin.

- Keep treats in a child-friendly container. You'll be less likely to dip into their treat box if it's emblazoned with kiddy cartoon characters.
- If late-night snacking when the kids are in bed is a habit, brush your teeth after dinner or try chewing gum.
- Kids love to crunch foods – so find some alternatives so your cupboards aren't packed full with tempting bags of crisps. Try roasting nuts in the oven, and then sprinkle with some soy sauce. They are delicious and full of good fats.
- Do your food shop on a full stomach. You'll be more likely to stick to the foods you need, and your children won't be throwing a tantrum if you don't buy the things that catch their eye.
- Try to break the cycle of giving your children chocolate or sweets to keep them quiet or as a reward. Buy them stickers or their favourite magazine instead.
- Make healthy eating fun for your kids – and yourself – with 'lollipop'-shaped foods like corn on the cob, chicken drumsticks and home-made vegetable kebabs.
- After a hard day looking after the kids, it's easy to feel that you deserve an alcoholic drink to wind down. Start seeing the calories in alcohol in the same way you view them in food. You may pass up that third or fourth glass if you remember that a large 250ml glass of wine is equivalent to a 228-calorie ice-cream cone and that – at 210 calories a pint – cider comes with the same calories as a sugar doughnut.
- Find some stylish trainers you will be happy to be seen in – so you will have the freedom to be more active – and also consider investing in some good sports bras which you don't mind wearing all day so you are ready to exercise if the opportunity arises.
- Don't be too hard on yourself. If you've had a bad day and eaten most of your toddler's chocolate buttons, don't use it as an excuse to give up on your plan altogether. There's

nothing wrong with a little bit of chocolate. It's hogging the whole family-size bag that's the problem. Remember it takes 3,500 calories to get an extra pound of body fat – so one unplanned cheat isn't a game-changer. Think of it as taking a 'time-out' – and then go back to healthy eating.

- If you can, go to bed earlier. With so much to do it's easy to get into a pattern of turning in at midnight – even though the kids are up at 6.30am. Often we eat for a pick-me-up when we're tired. If you are exhausted and overwhelmed, your self-control is the first thing to suffer.

Getting more time for yourself

When you have children, it's not just the sheer relentlessness that's so shocking. It's also the lack of time you have left for yourself.

One study estimated that new mothers have just 17 minutes of 'me' time a day.[24] By the time you've had a quick shower and brushed your hair, it's gone.

Although more men are staying at home to care for children, women are generally more likely to suffer from overload because they tend to be people-pleasers who put their own needs second.

For many mums, the downward spiral begins when they fall for the belief that they need to be constantly wired to get anything done.

Harvard stress counsellor Joan Borysenko, author of *Fried: Why You Burn Out and How to Revive* (Hay House, 2011), says that simple awareness can be the best protection. Joan says: 'Create a sliding scale in your head. At one end, the number one means "I'm feeling really good", and ten is "I'm feeling burnt out." Keep drawing a hatch line between those two points to work out where you stand. If it gets to an eight – and you're feeling like you can't stand it anymore – it's time to take a moment to relieve the situation.'[25]

Always keep in mind that you do not need to sacrifice everything to be a good mother – despite the messages society gives you. The more in balance you are, the better you will be at taking care of others. The happier you are, the happier your family is.

Ways to get more 'me time'

Cut your time drains. While mums are good multi-taskers, sometimes there are just too many tasks. Give yourself permission to be brutal about time-sapping people or activities. Practise politely saying no.

Draw boundaries. If you work, bosses and colleagues will keep pushing for as long as you keep giving. They won't give a thought as to whether the stress levels in your home are being raised by emailing and ringing you out of hours, during family time that traditionally would have been sacred. Establish boundaries by setting up auto-replies on your email and voicemail in the hours between school pick-up and bedtime.

Share the load. Make sure you are a genuine team with your partner. Maybe cooking is his strength, while finances are yours. Be interchangeable so that if one of you is taking a break, the other can easily slip into the other's shoes.

Take family holidays. The breaks we take as families are so often what people remember most clearly about their childhoods. Stepping away from the daily pressures of your everyday lives for a few days – and getting a break from technology – helps keep the bond between you and your child strong, and puts the fun back into your relationships.

Let off steam. Apart from exercise, one of the simplest – and most proven ways, for women in particular – to de-stress is to simply talk to friends in whom you can confide. If you complain to a partner, they are likely to feel guilty and semi-responsible – and think they have to come up with instant fixes. They may become more stressed themselves, because they will interpret you letting off steam as a sign that you can't cope, when what you really need is to release your pressure valve.

So find mums who are at the same stage as you. If you are home-based, attend the baby and toddler classes closest to you. That way you will have more chance of getting there regularly and it's less daunting. Try turning up every week so you become a regular face.

Just getting out of the house and having a change of scenery will do wonders for your frazzled state of mind.

Once children go to school, make a real effort to get friendly with other mums by arranging play-dates. Find two or three others in the same boat, and take each other's mobile numbers so that you can all step in and help each other out, as well as let off steam together.

Exercising with the kids in tow

The lack of time women get to themselves after they have children is the main reason it's so hard to go back to exercise.

This leaves us not only struggling to feel that we still have control over our body, but also missing out on a key way to reduce our stress levels.

To begin with at least, your best option is to make sure baby comes too. Think about getting a three-wheeler, all-terrain pram, which means you can power-walk and really pound the pavement. A 20-minute walk to the shops could burn up to 175 calories. If you need an extra boost, join a mum's buggy exercise programme at your nearest park.

Of course, this only works for as long as your child is young enough to stay put – and if you only have one in tow.

After that, change your attitude – and start thinking of a visit to the swings as some valuable exercise time you can share with your children as well as being fun for them.

Sometimes we make exercise far too much of a mountain. Remember when you were a child and you happily played outdoors? Chances are you adored every second and didn't consider it a big chore. Step back into that mindset. By using the play equipment like a gym circuit, you could burn up nearly 400 calories in an hour – the same as the average gym session – and entertain the kids at the same time.

The playground workout

Playing catch. This is a great warm-up to get you going. Uses biceps, triceps, shoulders and back muscles. In 10 minutes, you could burn 80 calories.

Swings. While you're pushing your child, extend your arms fully so you can feel your limbs stretch. Put your hands at the very edge of the swing seat to work all the muscles across the chest like a chest press. But don't get carried away, or your child will end up in the clouds. Try to alternate which arm you push with. Try both hands for 20 pushes, then 20 with each arm. This will exercise your chest, upper back and triceps. It will help rid you of your underarm 'bingo wings' and in five minutes you can burn 25 calories. If the playground is not packed and you don't feel like an idiot, try lunging too – you will also be working out your buttocks and thighs. With the lunges added, you will burn off an extra 20 calories.

See-saw. A see-saw can provide you with a great resistance exercise for your arms and chest. If your child has a playmate, put both of them on the see-saw. Then stand in front of the central pivot point. Bend over and put your palms on each side of the pivot about two feet apart. Do as many pushes as you can. When you get tired, have a quick rest but try to repeat three times. Use the front of your shoulders, triceps and chest. Five minutes will burn 30 calories.

If you're with a friend, another idea is to try sitting at opposite ends of the see-saw with your kids on your lap, and send each other up and down to give your thighs and buttocks a work-out. In 10 minutes, you will burn about 50 calories.

Slide. If your child weighs under 12kg, do some weightlifting by lifting him or her to the top of the slide. While she is sliding down, stand on the first rung of the ladder. Hold on for balance and raise up on to the balls of your feet, then slowly lower your heels as far as they can go. Go up and down on your toes to work your calves, remembering to support your back by drawing in your tummy. Repeat as many times as you can before your child comes back round for another turn. This uses back, bottom and calf muscles. Three sets of 12 lifts will burn about 20 calories.

Roundabout. As soon as you have lifted your child on and the roundabout is spinning, jog around the outside and pretend to chase her. Keep jogging until your child is ready to stop – or gets too dizzy. Try it for five minutes and you will burn about 40 calories.

Climbing frame. Now you are grown up, the horizontal bars are the perfect height for working out your back and arms. First try a chin-up. Put your hands shoulder-width apart. Grab the bar above you and hang by your arms, then try to pull your chin up towards the bar as you bend your arms. This will require a lot of strength so don't be surprised if you can hardly bend your arms at all. Come up as far as you can but don't strain yourself. Do this exercise for a minute then give yourself a full minute's rest. Next try some leg raises, which work out the abdominal muscles. Hang by your arms, bend your legs and raise your knees towards your body. Use the large muscles in your back and your abs. In 10 minutes, you will burn 50 calories.

Play tag. Take heart. More studies are showing that short bursts of exercise can be even more efficient at getting rid of fat. According to some research, just two and a half minutes of high-intensity interval training (HIIT), divided into five 30-second bursts, four minutes apart, was found to burn up to 220 calories.[26] So a regular, energetic game of tag really could help keep you in trim – as well as be amazing fun for the children.

And finally ... Another option for free exercise is to find one of the growing number of outdoor gyms. There are now over 200 in local parks up and down the country, installed by local councils. They feature all the usual equipment, from bench presses to exercise bikes. Go to tgogc.com to find out if there is one close by.

Other kid things you can do to keep fit

Trampolining. As well as being great fun to do with the kids, trampolining boosts everything from bone density to muscle tone and posture. For average-size women, it also burns about 200 calories an hour.

Skipping. Skipping improves your heart and lung fitness and makes bones and muscles strong. It also burns up more calories than any other popular exercise except for fast running. Ten minutes of moderate skipping burns 70 calories.

Hula-hooping. According to the American Council on Exercise, you should burn approximately 200 calories if you hula-hoop for 30 minutes. It's also great for posture, your pelvic floor and tightening up your abdominal muscles.

Cycling. Balance bikes mean kids are learning to cycle earlier than ever – so get on your bike too. It's a great family activity that can help you – and them – keep fit throughout their childhood.

Exercising without the kids

Getting into an exercise routine can seem daunting when you feel shattered anyway.

But, ultimately, exercising regularly can give you more energy, help you sleep better and combat anxiety and stress, so it's well worth making it a priority.

For home-based mums, joining an evening class can also be a valuable chance to get out of the house without the kids in tow.

A proven method of bringing your stress levels down several notches is yoga. As well as keeping you fit and toned, and a good way to get back into exercise again after birth, it improves your breathing, relieves physical tension and gives you a mental escape into the bargain. Indeed, according to Harvard University researchers yoga is a particularly good way of learning how to regulate your stress response system – perfect if you are an overworked mother.[27]

It's also fabulously flexible because you can start doing yoga with your baby, find a class that offers a crèche when they get wrigglier, and swap babysitting credits with a friend so you can both take turns going. Yoga classes can also range from gentle to much more challenging, so you can choose the style and level which best suits you. You also have a good chance of keeping yoga up because you can do it so easily at home with nothing more than a basic mat – once you're familiar with the poses. Pilates shares many of the same benefits but with more emphasis on core strength, and less on the mind-clearing aspects of yoga.

Whatever your exercise of choice, don't forget that YouTube is a huge bonus for time-starved mums because it offers exercise videos of every conceivable length that you can follow along with. It means there is always one of a suitable length to squeeze into a child's naptime or whatever window becomes free in your day. Even if you only grab 10 or 15 minutes at a time, it all adds up. And according to HIIT experts, working out for short sharp bursts is the way to go, so in 10 minutes you can achieve a lot.

How to get more support

You are not a superhero. With the best will in the world, you cannot do this all on your own. Trying to appear the perfect parent who has it all under control, when really you are a swan desperately paddling under the surface, only piles the pressure on yourself to keep up appearances.

There is no shame in admitting you can't do everything. The social shifts over the last 20 to 30 years – more households in which both parents work, fragmented families and more demanding work schedules – mean that we're often expected to take on a burden that at times can become too much.

In the words of the African proverb, it really does take a village to raise a child. Take deliberate steps to build a supportive network of people – friends, neighbours or relations – not only to help you out in an emergency, but who also know your child well enough to be loving care-givers – and allow you to recharge your batteries once in a while.

Grandparents

Parents can forget very quickly what it's like to be working when you've got young children. It's also easy to forget that throughout most of history children have been brought up by their extended family – not just by one exhausted parent.

It may be that grandparents haven't suggested helping simply because they feel hesitant about interfering or don't realise how much pressure you are under. They may also not feel confident about looking after a young child after a long break from childcare – or worried that you may not like their style. They may simply believe they've done their bit.

Don't be a martyr. But do point out that your child's family doesn't just end with you and your partner. Explain to both your parents and your parents-in-law that times have got tougher, you have a lot on your plate – and that you may need help.

Get into good habits from the start – or get them involved – so they get some practice. Never exploit them or ever take them for granted. But make them feel needed by telling them you would much rather your child was looked after by a family member in an emergency. Suggest they could also improve your parenting by occasionally giving you a break to give you some time to recharge your batteries.

If they are willing to help, communication will be the key. Think through any difference of opinion or parenting philosophies. Agree first on the main issues to do with sleep and diet. But don't assume that everything they have to say is outdated because, after all, they will have more experience as well as a longer-term perspective.

Neighbours, friends and fellow mums

With babysitting fees now rising far quicker than general salaries, hiring a babysitter can cost a small fortune. Getting organised with a babysitting circle is one of the best ways to have a ready-made set of carers on tap – and for no cost.

If there isn't one at the school or playgroup or in your road, start one by asking some of the mums near you for coffee and let it build from there. The best number is between seven and 12 mums, so that it's a manageable number, and children always have a familiar face. It helps to have parents who have kids with similar ages so your needs are all roughly the same.

Then work out a voucher system. Each time you babysit for another member of the circle, you receive a token – and you lose one when someone babysits for you. If that sounds like too much administration, you could arrange a more informal set-up among three or four close friends and swap credits for date nights or for other types of 'me time'.

Making time for your partner

The real risk to a couple's relationship often comes from the rising stress levels that start to build up in the home as a result of the hectic schedules that evolve when parents aim to maximise every moment of their child's life.

As extracurricular activities, from drama to gym, start to get more serious as children get older, they start to leach into the weekend. The result is that instead of spending time together, couples end up acting as if they were in a never-ending relay race, passing the baton, and being a taxi service between various activities. This rush, rush, rush atmosphere at the very time of the week when families need to spend time together inevitably causes rows.

But the best gift you can give your kids is a stable relationship – and that demands quality 'couple time'. You may be juggling a lot of balls – but don't let your relationship come last. It's the bedrock of your family's security.

Be inventive. Most of us are too exhausted to think of anything but sleep by the time we get to bed. So get intimate at unusual times of the day, like in the morning before the kids wake up and during nap times. Set an alarm if you have to.

Bring the kids. You don't have to leave the kids out to have some romance. In fact, it's good for your kids to see you looking happy and relaxed together. At weekends, get out of the house as a family – even if it's just for a long walk in the park where you can hold hands while the children play. Sometimes all it takes is a change of scenery away from the distractions and busy-ness of home to feel a bit closer as a couple.

Stay on the same side. Put on a united front. Even if you disagree behind closed doors about a childrearing issue, don't argue about it in front of the children or it will cause resentment between you – and your children won't respect either of you. If you want to iron out an issue, don't do it in the heat of the moment, but when you are removed from the flashpoint and able to listen to each other calmly.

Support your partner's parenting. When your partner is in charge of the children, agree on your general values first but otherwise let them do it their own way. Give praise for what they do well, rather than criticise. Over time, criticism can have a corrosive effect on your relationship.

Turn off the screens. You may think you're relaxing together at the end of the day if you are sitting side by side with your laptops on the sofa. But you might as well be communicating across a brick wall – because it's unlikely that you are really listening or connecting. Make a commitment to give each other a thorough debrief on each other's days – and put the phones and computers away. Otherwise it does not take long for a creeping separateness to seep into your relationship.

Look after the minutes. Even the simplest gestures can add up over the week. When you're busy with work and children, often it's a question of finding mere minutes together rather than hours. A hug in the morning and in the evening and a thoughtful text all add up – and still make you feel close even if you're not seeing much of each other.

Don't generalise. Try never to say 'you always' or 'you never' to your partner. There is nothing more irritating. And just like kids, if partners feel 'labelled' they give up trying to change.

Have a home dinner date. Even if you can't afford a date night at a restaurant or a babysitter, once the kids are in bed, order a takeaway, put away the phones and have a date. Or swap babysitting credits with friends so you are not stressed by the cost of going out for the evening. Ring-fencing time for each other keeps you communicating as a couple – not just as parents. Try to make it once a week and put it in your diary.

Conclusion

It would be a tragedy if you looked back at your children's childhood and all you remembered was rushing from A to B, bundling them off to school so you could get to work, or drowning in household chores. Imagine too if that was what your children remembered most when they looked back on their childhood in 20 years' time.

I wrote this book because today's culture of busy-ness is taking the joy out of parenting and the fun out of childhood. I wrote it because I fear the too-much-to-do culture is stealing away the best moments of our lives.

Among the many different life hacks and strategies here, I hope you have found a few eureka moments to help you streamline your life and cut out some of the irritating frustrations that make a demanding job even more challenging.

If it's enabled you to spend any more uninterrupted, more relaxed time with your child, rather than feeling stalked by your to-do list, this book has achieved its goal. Keep using it to find as much time for your children as you can.

There is no perfectly prepared meal, no freshly ironed outfit or spotless kitchen floor that can equal the hours and minutes you spend with them.

Sources

1   Office of National Statistics (ONS), 2014.

2   ONS, 2013.

3   ONS, December 2011.

4   'Parents "spend just 34 minutes a day quality time with their children" – because stressful life is too distracting'. Based on a poll of 10,000 families by Highland Spring. *Daily Mirror*, 14 April 2015.

5   'It's curtains for bedtime stories: Study reveals that one in five parents don't read a story to their children'. Based on a poll of 2,000 parents by Fox 2000 Pictures. *Daily Mail*, 11 July 2014.

6   'Parents and children spend less than an hour with each other every day because of modern demands'. Based on a poll of 2,000 parents by Virgin Resorts. *Daily Mail*, 13 July 2013. Also see 'Working parents feel they neglect children: Almost half worry they are not good enough parents and have just half an hour of time for their children a night', a study of 2,000 parents by OnePoll, 24 April 2013.

7   IKEA *Play Report*, based on a global survey of 30,000 parents, 2015.

8   David Code, *Kids Pick Up On EVERYTHING: How Parental Stress is Toxic to Kids*, Createspace, 2011. For more on how parental stress is contagious to children, see 'Early childhood aetiology of mental health problems: a longitudinal population-based study', *Journal of Child Psychology and Psychiatry*, July 2008.

9   Michael Meany and Moshe Szyf, 'Environmental programming of stress responses through DNA methylation: life at the interface between a dynamic environment and a fixed genome', *Dialogues of Clinical Neuroscience*, 2005.

10 David Elkind, *The Hurried Child*, Da Capo Press, 2006.

11 'How does YOUR day compare? The average woman completes 59 tasks every day (including tidying, cleaning and nagging)'. Based on a poll of 1,583 mothers of school-age children. *Daily Mail*, 2 December 2015. Nine out of 10 mothers polled said that they take the lead when it comes to all

child-related household tasks, and seven in 10 often feel overwhelmed by the amount they have to remember each day.

12 Rob Parsons, *The Sixty Minute Family: An Hour to Transform Your Relationships for Ever*, Lion, 2010.

13 'Nutritional comparison of fresh, frozen and canned fruits and vegetables', *Journal of the Science of Food and Agriculture*, 2007. See also 'Don't sneer at canned food! Even rice pud's nutritious', Angela Dowden, *Daily Mail*, 3 November 2015.

14 Study of 26,000 children aged between 11 and 15 by psychiatrists at Canada's McGill University, published in the *Journal of Adolescent Health*, March 2013.

15 Interview with Jackie Marsh by Anthony Harwood for the *Daily Telegraph*, November 2015.

16 John Medina, *Brain Rules for Baby: How to Raise a Smart and Happy Child from Zero to Five*, Pear Press, 2012.

17 'How does YOUR day compare? The average woman completes 59 tasks every day (including tidying, cleaning and nagging)'. Based on a poll of 1,583 mothers of school-age children. *Daily Mail*, 2 December 2015.

18 'The tyranny of the Tiger Mother: Exhausted children are "working" for more than 54 hours a week'. Based on a survey of 2,000 parents by Haliborange. *Daily Mail*, 5 September 2013.

19 Unicef, *Report on Child Well-Being*, 2011. Also see 'How much children own' discussed in 'What really makes our children happy?', *Sunday Telegraph*, 18 September 2011.

20 Jeffrey Froh, 'Gratitude and the reduced costs of materialism in adolescents', *Journal of Happiness Studies*, March 2010.

21 Dr Rebecca Scharf, 'Nighttime Sleep Duration and Externalizing Behaviors of Preschool Children', *Journal of Developmental and Behavioral Pediatrics*, July 2013.

22 'The new-mom body survey'. Based on a survey of 7,000 women by Babycenter.com, April 2013.

23 Researchers from the University of Chicago followed 774 women with an average body mass index in the 'overweight' range. They found

that more than 75% of them weighed more one year after giving birth than they did pre-pregnancy. Published in the *Journal of Obstetrics and Gynaecology*, December 2014.

24 Based on a survey of 2,000 mothers. *Daily Mail*, 5 February 2014.

25 Joan Borysenko, *Fried: Why You Burn Out and How to Revive*, Hay House, 2011.

26 Based on research presented at the Integrative Biology of Exercise VI meeting, Colorado, October 2013.

27 'Yoga for anxiety and depression', *Harvard Mental Health Letter*, April 2009.

Recommended reading

Benson, Peter, *Sparks: How Parents Can Ignite the Hidden Strengths of Teenagers*, Jossey Bass, 2008

Borysenko, Joan, *Fried: Why You Burn Out and How to Revive*, Hay House, 2011

Carey, Tanith, *Girls, Uninterrupted: Steps for Building Stronger Girls in a Challenging World*, Icon, 2015

Carey, Tanith, *Taming the Tiger Parent*, Constable/Little Brown, 2014

Cave, Simone and Fertleman, Caroline, *Potty Training Boys and Potty Training Girls*, Vermilion, 2008

Cave, Simone and Fertleman, Caroline, *Coping with Two*, Hay House, 2012

Chachamu, Miriam, *How to Calm a Challenging Child*, Foulsham, 2008

Code, David, *Kids Pick Up On EVERYTHING: How Parental Stress is Toxic to Kids*, Createspace, 2011

Elkind, David, *The Hurried Child*, Da Capo Press, 2006

Hodgkinson, Tom, *The Idle Parent: Why Less Means More When Raising Kids*, Penguin, 2010

Honoré, Carl, *Under Pressure: Putting the Child Back In Childhood*, Orion, 2009

McCosker, Kim and Bermingham, Rachael, *Four Ingredients*, 4 Ingredients Publishing, 2008

Morris, Jayne, *Burnout to Brilliance: Strategies for Sustainable Success*, Changemakers Books, 2015

Janis-Norton, Noël, *Calmer, Easier, Happier Homework: The Revolutionary Programme That Transforms Homework*, Hodder & Stoughton, 2013

Janis-Norton, Noël, *Calmer, Easier, Happier Parenting: The Revolutionary Programme That Transforms Family Life*, Hodder & Stoughton, 2012 (For courses with Noël, go to www.tnlc.info)

Medina, John, *Brain Rules for Baby: How to Raise a Smart and Happy Child from Zero to Five*, Pear Press, 2012

Parsons, Rob, *The Sixty Minute Family: An Hour To Transform Your Relationships for Ever*, Lion Books, 2010

Runkel, Hal, *Screamfree Parenting: The Revolutionary Approach to Raising Your Kids by Keeping Your Cool*, Broadway Books, 2009

Smart, Denise, *Meal in a Mug: 80 Fast, Easy Recipes for Hungry People – All You Need is a Mug and a Microwave*, Ebury, 2014

Taylor, Charlie, *Divas and Dictators: The Secrets to Having a Much Better Behaved Child*, Vermilion, 2009

Index

Index

Index